NEW GIRL LAW

DRAFTING A FUTURE FOR CAMBODIA

ANNE ELIZABETH MOORE

DRAFTING A FUTURE FOR CAMBODIA

Part 2 of a 4 part series.

Anne Elizabeth Moore

Released March 31, 2013
First printing
ISBN 9781621064626
Cantankerous Titles #9

Cover by Mari Naomi
Fonts by Ian Lynam
Designed by Joe Biel
Edited by Joe Biel

Distributed by IPG, Chicago and Turnaround, UK

Cantankerous Titles
636 SE 11th Ave.
Portland, OR 97214

An imprint of Microcosm Publishing

www.microcosmpublishing.com
www.cantankeroustitles.com

For those who have been shamed, but speak anyway
and for the rest of you, who must be articulate in silence.

Contents

PROLOGUE

There exists a theory (and I'll admit it's a batty one) that certain geographical locations lack the requisite gravitational force to operate within the bounds of physics, and thus exert an increase in social pressures. In such spaces, it is believed, physical integrity can only be preserved through political domination. Without tyranny, all constituents, all inhabitants would fly off in all directions. Carefree and happy, but uninvested, loose. Everyone off on his or her own. No resources, no reason to return. Nothing has tied people together, no one is connected to anything. Wasted mass, unharnessed force— if a tree falls in the woods but everything flies off into the furthest recesses of space sort of thing.

In terms of the physical sciences, but also the social sciences, and probably even the junk sciences, the theory doesn't hold a lot of water. It's actually fiction, like *pure fiction*, invented by short-story writer Etgar Keret in the process of making things up about the world that are charming and fantastic but hold little place in our world of provable truth, the evolution of facts, quotidian existence. The theory cannot ever be proven and doesn't even really exist *as theory*, it's just written down. Sorry. I admit I only wrote *theory* so you would try to believe it for a second before you realized that it probably didn't make any sense, which it probably wouldn't, unless you have been to Phnom Penh.

It is frequently the case that veracity depends on its environment. Something that does not seem true elsewhere may prove irrefutable on the Rosebud Reservation in South Dakota, say, or in a nearly empty café one night in the Mitte in Berlin, or under a sleeping kitten, for whom you are acting as a mattress. It is not objectively verifiable, for example, that ghosts exist everywhere, that he will love you forever, or that everything is now and will always be just fine. But these statements are true in these moments, facts contingent on location. It can be enough, even if science cannot allow for relative, site-specific truths.

Cambodia lacks a kind of gravity. It always has. It is not a historical problem, nor one put in place by any particular government. It is not the fault of the Khmer Rouge, and Americans did not enforce it, neither the

French or the Vietnamese. It is not caused by a lack of minerals in the floodplains or the rice-ready soil. It's just that inhabitants may wander off at any moment, unhindered by duties or necessity or anything, only compelled by the beauty of a fold of cloth, a certain arm's small gesture, an awkward but traditional key change that brings to mind a wedding, a birth, a funeral. The only explanation is that the region simply has lesser amounts of a single natural resource, requiring a force and a fury to weight those who live there against oblivion.

At least, this is the only explanation that makes sense, if you know anything about the country.

•   •   •

Little is clear about the area now known as Cambodia before the 9th century, but over the course of the next three hundred years, the kingdom of Angkor grew into a mighty empire that dominated much of the Mekong river region, with only occasional lapses. The famed temples—you can see one on the flag—stand as a testament to Khmer irrigational and architectural ingenuity. They are metaphors for military strength as well as domestic, likely forced, labor.

Thais sacked Angkor in 1431, absconding with many of the intellectual and cultural elite. The remaining of these classes migrated south to Phnom Penh, where they eventually settled the new capital as the empire weakened. Between 1600 and 1863, a series of inefficient kings presided over the struggling nation, who bolstered efforts with alliances shifting easily from Thailand to Vietnam and back again, each fostering a variety of occupation we don't call colonialism because not European. (Today, border disputes still arise—is it any wonder?—and the languages melt, one into the other. Flashes of anger, ancient but raw, are still on display sometimes over the design of a t-shirt or the placement of a sign.)

The period of invitational colonization ended in 1864 with actual French colonialism, from the colonial era and everything, when King Norodom I signed a treaty of protectorate in an effort to cede borders no further to its neighbors. Within two decades, the country was largely under French administration. More kings came after, with no change in status for the nation now remote-controlled, until 1941, when Norodom Sihanouk was crowned king at the age of 19. It was thought that he would be amenable to French interests, but by 1954 he had successfully gained independence for Cambodia. In a brilliant political maneuver, Sihanouk stepped down from the throne the following year, created a political party, and was installed into parliament, from where he continued to dominate Cambodian politics for another decade and a half. He declared his newly independent country a neutral territory, thus giving up U.S. aid, from which much of his military funding had come. It didn't mean, however, that he ended diplomatic relations with the North Vietnamese and Chinese governments: When the War of U.S. Aggression (as the Vietnamese call it) or the Vietnam War (as we call it here) spilled into Cambodia's already trampled rice paddies, the king could not have been wholly surprised. His domestic maneuverings were also coming under attack, as corruption and political repression grew. In 1970, he was deposed as chief of state, and the U.S.-backed General Lon Nol and Prince Sisowath Sirik Matak, Sihanouk's cousin, were installed as replacements. For five years, civil war simmered. American bombings, unofficially begun in the late 1960s, continued. Hundreds of thousands died from attacks; more from starvation when their cattle were hit. Poverty did what poverty always does: made everything harder. Then the Khmer Rouge seized Phnom Penh.

This is history you may be more familiar with. Between April 17, 1975 and the very early days of 1979, between 1.7 and 2.2 million people died of exhaustion, starvation, and murder under ultra-communist Democratic Kampuchea. A Vietnamese invasion ended the regime, but started a new occupation: Until 1989 the Vietnamese-backed People's Republic of Kampuchea ruled the nation. Resistance remained strong, however, and the Khmer Rouge, hiding in the jungle, were among several groups continuing to wage civil war throughout the country.

In the early 1990s, UNTAC, the United Nations Transitional Authority in Cambodia, took over administration of the government. It organized and ran the country's first democratic election and managed its own radio station and jail—the first time the UN had gone beyond monitoring and supervising in-place elections to effectively run a country. By most present-day accounts, it was a disaster: UNTAC workers had stipends some hundreds of times the average Cambodian annual income, and thrill-seeking journalists looking for drugs and prostitutes became common sights on the streets of Phnom Penh. Name-brand cigarette smoking and alcohol consumption, spurred by a dramatic increase in advertising, flourished. Not to mention that the presence of the UN Peacekeeping forces did little to quell violence, even giving warring factions decision-making power in the administration of the country. Civil war continued until 1999. The UN did, smartly, give everyone radios. Many are still in use today, and remain one of the only ways Cambodians receive a diversity of opinions on political matters, as most television and Khmer-language newspapers are aligned with the ruling party.

The democratic election process did take—sort of. The Cambodian People's Party, led by now-Prime Minister Hun Sen, a former Khmer Rouge cadre then appointed to the ministry under the People's Republic of Kampuchea, has dominated Cambodian politics since 1993, despite allegations of violence and corruption at the polls. Local elections began to install representatives to villages and communes in 2002, but the appearance of democracy can be deceiving. We don't call it colonialism because we call it the free market, but use of the U.S. Dollar has nearly replaced the Cambodian Riel in urban areas over the last ten years.

Dizzying, isn't it? It makes you light-headed just to think about. Physics can't explain it, but things work differently in the Kingdom of Cambodia.

•　　•　　•

By January 1, 2008, I was living in what I will call the Euglossa Dormitory for University Women in Phnom Penh, Cambodia for six weeks. (The names of all individuals and organizations, and most distinguishing characteristics, have been changed in this text. The events are described as I remember or experienced them; in some cases, however, you will note that there is information I simply did not seek out.) The date was important to me. I thought of it as New Year's Day, and celebrated it as the end of one adventure and the beginning of another. The date was not important to my young Khmer sisters. They thought of it as American New Year which, since it did not align with Cambodian New Year in the middle of April, meant there was something basically wrong with Americans, particularly in regards to how they thought about time. My birthday was right around the Cambodian New Year, and I adored the residents of Euglossa without restriction, so I was susceptible to their arguments.

I had originally been invited to the country by the dorm's founder, a delightful American entrepreneur that I respected and enjoyed. My friend Caroline, a Chicago-based social-justice advocate that used to live in Phnom Penh, had introduced me to him. His project struck both of us at the time as a deeply rooted, thoughtful response to Cambodia's longstanding gender problem. A centuries-old tradition had kept young women from renting property, living alone in the city, or even finishing high school. Building a dormitory that gave women space to live while they attended college was a clever, supportive response to Cambodia's own struggle to rebuild.

At the time, the country was beginning to shed notions of itself as *poor* and had begun referring to itself as *developing*. You could see it, sometimes, in the middle of sentences. Elders would correct themselves in conversation, responding to foreigners' queries with, "But in Cambodia, is not the same. We are a poor country—maybe we develop now. We are a developing country."

Development was taking many forms, however. The most obvious was physical: New buildings, more elaborate even than Gold Tower 42, were being planned. New developments. Skyscrapers, fast food outlets, and luxury hotels put up at a dizzying pace, sometimes faster than those who lived on the land were prepared for. Mass evictions continued, were contested on legal grounds, usually went through anyway. Cambodia, where mass poverty had always been a problem, could begin to identify specific areas of concern, and foster non-governmental organizations, or NGOs, to address each: Urban homelessness, labor, graft and corruption, corporate greed. Education became a primary concern, and organizations like Euglossa were attracting attention. New paradigms emerged or took hold: Morality. Nationalism. Identity. Neoliberalism. Class war.

Development meant other concerns could come to the fore: cultural concerns. A new law banned songs with explicitly adulterous themes from karaoke bars, an attempt to strengthen monogamy through legislation. Yet the songs targeted were of a specific breed—all popular songs by female vocalists narrating attempts to lure married men into bed. "If I Can't be First Can I be Second," "Love Another's Husband," and "May I Have a Piece of Your Heart Too." The new legislation was also, few noted, an attempt to control the public expression of female sexual desire.

Stringent control over Cambodian women was not new. But the young Khmer women I knew were beginning to identify and resist it.

•   •   •

The original project that brought me to Cambodia, chronicled in *Cambodian Grrrl: Self-Publishing in Phnom Penh,* was complete by the new year. I'd taught thirty-two future leaders the practice of self-publishing, and with their newfound skills they had begun chronicling their own lives and piece together their own histories—histories otherwise untold in Khmer text books, around the family dinner table, or in newspapers, due to the mass of conflicting traumas from every memorable era. We had also, collectively, begun implementing both local and international distribution programs, so that these young women were not only documenting history for themselves, but sharing their experiences with others. The little booklets we made were *zines*—short for *fanzines*, editions of self-published text and images that I'd been making in the U.S. since before the 17, 18, and 19 year-olds I was working with were born.

It was challenging work in a largely illiterate culture. My devotion to self-publishing as a noncommercial mode of expression, in a developing country with strict government controls over freedom of speech, compounded the difficulties. The young women of Euglossa, my trusting Cambodian sisters, never questioned how media could be a tool for social justice. Yet questions about how we published their zines safely, why we didn't sell them, what made people want to read them, and why I didn't start an NGO so I could get paid to do this work hounded me whenever I left the dorm.

The first question was easy to answer. We published in English, didn't directly challenge the government, and distributed zines by hand. That's how we did it safely. (We also enjoyed the natural protection of being mostly Cambodian women—presumed, maybe even more than was justified, to be silent. To boot, there was also the unassailable fact that we simply weren't being critical.) The second question I usually waffled on. In a poor country, where few read—even fewer in English—a domestic readership was hard enough to build without charging folks, too. At least, that's what I told people.

The real reason we didn't sell our zines was more complicated. In short, money was less important than creating a space, however small, to speak a previously unuttered truth. Beyond that, however, stands the acknowledgment that the truths of women, particularly from and in developing nations, just don't sell. That's what I was hearing almost every day from editors I pitched stories to at publications back home. (Later, when I was writing on garment workers, the logic clarified: no one wants to know how their clothes get made, I was given to understand.) I didn't want this group of young women to be forced to measure the value of their work along a commercial scale, particularly one designed to take advantage of the desperate needs of women in developing nations. Too, as the Kingdom developed, money was becoming a flash point for almost everything, certainly including government scrutiny. There was no reason to draw attention to the fact that we had stopped being silent—and the perception that we might be profiting from our work would do just that.

So we practiced speaking out, but noted with some care the pressures to remain quiet. The forces that shame and humiliate women into silence around the world usually go unwritten. In Cambodia, they were available at every bookstall in town.

. . .

Committed to paper sometime in the mid-1800's, the *Chbap Srei* is a didactic text—its title translates literally to *Girl Law*, or *Rules for Girls*. Its intention is to outline a strict code of conduct for women. Alongside its shorter sibling— *Chbap Bros*, or *Rules for Men*—the text acts as a normative poem, not unlike a commercial jingle. Both rulebooks were likely passed down orally for generations before finding their way to the page.

Historian David Chandler, in a 1984 volume of the *Journal of Southeast Asian Studies*, cautions against interpreting such texts too literally. He explains that they "provide an idealized picture, suggesting norms of behavior rather than describing or analyzing the ways in which people behave." He also allows that their status as texts in a "largely illiterate society… pass[es] on the ideology of a minority elite," conceding however that "this may be a circular argument, brought on by the widespread popularity… of the chbap themselves." They're not journalistic accounts of pre-colonial life, in other words: They're prescriptive texts intended to guide social behavior. Yet the degree to which they worked is not known.

They were very popular, and in use for a long time. Chandler goes on: "For several centuries they celebrated the sociability, politeness, and repetitions of family life." Now, he says, "Like the villages they served, the chbap themselves have been abandoned."

Foreign journalists and social workers and women's rights advocates I was meeting in the early days of 2008 agreed: The *Chbap Srei* was old news. Ancient history. No longer relevant. The girls I was living with simply weren't affected by it, university professors and ex-pats explained. Certainly, village life had been destroyed: The CIA had identified it as a barrier to American interests back when Sihanouk was king, according to William Shawcross in *Sideshow*. The bombing campaign, Lon Nol, and UNTAC had certainly changed the way people operated outside of the capital. Still, that didn't mean the chbaps were gone. *Where could I see a copy?* I asked one ex-pat working in mental health services. *You'll never find one,* she told me. *They just don't print them anymore.*

I took an interest in the dorm residents' book collections, although I could not read through them, and began to note a silence that would arise around certain texts. So although the Euglossa girls, too, told me that the *Chbap Srei* "didn't affect to them," I once asked if anyone had a copy.

"Of *course*," they said, in that exaggerated way that respectfully and lovingly implied I was an imbecile for having asked. Almost every one of the thirty-two residents had their own copies of the supposedly irrelevant text, and when I asked my roommate Amoun to bring me shopping to find my own, we located several versions, at each bookstall we visited, to choose from.

Still, no one would translate it for me. "It bad," Dara told me, in her very unsure English and tiny soft voice. Her name meant *star*, and she did shine, but she spoke only when necessary. "We think you don't want to know," the level-headed Kimlong explained finally, adjusting her wire-rimmed glasses.

But I did. The most easily accessible English translation of the *Chbap Srei* was conducted by Dr. Mai of the Partnership Against Domestic Violence Cambodia and posted on a French blog called *Carpediem'ilia*. The advice the text gives, as Chandler asserts, is pretty simple: To be a good

Cambodian woman, remain quiet, respectful, and pliable. This sounds fine until we get down to the specifics of what that means, a spate of prescriptives that often include admonishments to remain fearful, silent, and lesser-than. "No matter how poor you are, follow the woman's rules. If you don't feel afraid of your husband's feeling... we call you a woman who lacks a good characteristic," is one example.

About this husband, further advice is required: "Serve well and don't make him disappointed... don't speak in the way that you consider him as equal. No matter what happen he says, even if it's bad, we have to listen. Though your husband speaks inappropriately you shouldn't let the mother know."

Not the husband's mother, certainly. Not the wife's, either. In fact, remain silent about all matters of family life. "My dear, no matter what your husband did wrong, I tell you to be patient, don't say anything without the husband present. Don't curse, don't be the enemy, no matter how poor or stupid: Don't look down on him.... You should be patient with him and calm down your anger."

About women who do not tamp their rage, much is specified. The sorrow of women who express anger never ends, the text explains. "She simply spreads it around the village and it comes back to her, all the time." It is advisable to eliminate the feeling entirely, in fact, and not misdirect it toward the dog or the cat. A woman who does this "ruins the prestige of the family." True, excessive anger may be undesirable as well as unhealthy—certainly, Buddhists might prefer it be allowed to dissipate, too—but the *Chbap Srei* condemns other forms of expression for women as well:

> Another kind of girl, when she sleeps she turn her back to her husband. This one we consider as a bad snake and it shouldn't be let into the house.... The other kind of woman kicking something loudly. When she walk very loudly they consider her step like a lightening sound so that her skirt is torn apart. She walks very loudly so that the houses tremble. The other woman see something on the ground and then she move forward without cleaning it up: In the future she cannot get organized and her property will be lost.

In sum, the text offers few outlets for women to express themselves at all. However much it does lay out a perhaps over-idealized prescription for peaceful home life, the thrust of the *Chbap Srei* is this: Selfishness is not good, anger is not good, backtalk is not good, in fact talking at all might not be good. Fearlessness is definitely not good. Subservience, silence, and obedience are good.

It was an oppressive set of rules, but it was familiar. The only way I have found to explain the pressure to adhere to the rules of the *Chbap Srei* to American women and girls is by asking them this: What if advertising in the U.S. carried the weight of law?

•   •   •

In Cambodia, advertising was a sign of progress. The first billboard I remember seeing in the country was in 2007, for a Kentucky Fried Chicken that would open later in 2008. From the time the sign advertising it went to up to the time the fast-food chain opened (the nation's first major U.S. brand that was not bootlegged), billboards proliferated, like that crazy hoof and mouth disease would, a few years later.

It was distressing how quickly it happened, considering that the practice was totally illegal twenty-one years beforehand. Under the Vietnamese from 1979 until 1993, advertising was initially banned. Foreign media, too, until 1986. But the following year, Samdech Hun Sen—then only a former Khmer Rouge cadre making a name for himself in the People's Republic of Kampuchea—announced that advertising was now welcome on the radio.

The radio giveaway program UNTAC undertook in the early 1990s may have inspired a renewed interest in media, and claims of democracy certainly ring hollow without a vibrant press. Around thirty papers existed by the time UNTAC ended. This went up to forty-five the following year, which then doubled in 1995. By 2008, around three hundred newspapers, thirty newsletters, nearly a hundred magazines, and perhaps fifty varieties of international print media were listed on the Ministry of Information's official tally.

Still, radio remained the most significant source of news. A 2008 report by human rights group LICADHO found that only nine percent of polled subjects read a newspaper every day, and only *point three percent* of the population had Internet access. (A market research group a few years later found that only twelve percent of eleven hundred Cambodians polled regularly accessed the Internet, most of them wealthy young students in Phnom Penh. The same report found that one hundred percent of those polled watch television every day—those without electricity pop down to bars or coffeeshops to check in, although television is primarily seen as an entertainment medium, and not a news delivery service.)

Now, media can exist without advertising. Our zines were one example. And ads could exist without media—in fact they would need to, if they intended to attract the lucrative dollars of tourists, who rarely glance at Khmer-language media. Ads without media means: public signage.

In a 1996 study published in the trade mag *Tobacco Control,* Marshall Smith did a study of cigarette advertising in Phnom Penh that considered a total of nearly eighty-five hundred signs. He found that almost half of them were for tobacco products; about a third advertised alcohol; close to ten percent advertised non-alcoholic soft drinks; and the remainder were split between various consumer products and the name of the business operating at that location. At the time, a new law was about to go into effect, which limited tobacco advertising based on the designation, size, and placement of the sign. Under this new law, ads for tobacco products would be restricted from certain public areas. So tobacco companies found new ways to advertise in the late 1990s that were not restricted by these rules. They began handing out umbrellas, t-shirts, posters, flyers, and other items with logos on them. Sometimes the companies paid vendors for the advertising space, and sometimes the posters and ads were given away for free. Sometimes, however, the vendors or cyclo drivers (tuk-tuks were not yet available) *paid* for them, because even in that short time, advertising had come to symbolize the prestige of development.

Of course the question always arises, *Does advertising even matter?* The numbers here are clear. In Cambodia in 1996, half the signs tallied were for cigarettes and more than half (sixty-five percent) of adult men in Phnom Penh smoked. In Siem Reap this number was even higher. Another study by Marshall Smith, released a few years later in the same publication although conducted around the same time, looked exclusively at smoking in monks. A full three percent claimed they started smoking just because they saw it in an ad, but another twenty-one percent started due other marketing strategies: They were given free cigarettes by folks who normally sold them.

So almost a quarter of all the monks who smoked in 1996—an issue of globalization already, as many people felt that smoking was a violation of Buddhist precepts—said they smoked because of advertising and marketing.

In 2010 I would return to Phnom Penh and conduct my own study of advertising. A couple university students and I focused on a central area of Phnom Penh, near City Mall. We counted thirty-eight ads in a two-block radius. Over fifteen percent were for financial services, and a similar amount were for fast food or Western-style coffeeshops. Over ten percent were for high-end fashion goods. Nearly eight percent were for electronics. Slightly more than five percent were for soft drinks. The rest were for cell phones, cigarettes, and local businesses.

Of these, exactly half were signs for goods or services offered or produced on site. A quarter were second-party signs, for goods or services you could purchase on site, but that had been made elsewhere. And another quarter of these signs were for internationally-owned companies with no local representation at all. (It is one thing, as my students and I discussed, to sell fashion and hair products back to the young women that made them in the first place. A weird thing, perhaps, but it happens. It is another thing, however, to sell more expensive goods to a nation emerging from poverty if you haven't even given people jobs first.)

Together, the students conservatively estimated that a young person may go to and from school or work every day, ten blocks each way, and see three hundred and eighty ads. They may watch two hours of TV, which may add another twenty ads. The radio is on in the morning and maybe they will hear another twenty ads that way. A student may get three text messages per day on various cell phones that are ads for their own SIM card companies. He or she may go on the Internet for about an hour and see fifty ads on Facebook, Google, Yahoo, or whatever other sites they look at. On their way home someone may hand them a flyer. If a student looks through a magazine before he or she goes to bed, there could be fifty ads in it. So although it is a very rough estimate, we agreed that it seemed easy to approach viewing about five hundred ads per day.

Some students balked at the high number, and said, "Oh no. That is too many ads. There is no way we see that many ads in one day." We then watched two karaoke videos together and counted thirty different ads in and between them, in the space of about seven minutes. (Karaoke videos often include banner text ads across the bottom of the screen.) I asked them to spend a few days counting the number of ads they thought they saw each day, and afterwards many suggested that, after all, five hundred was too low an estimate for young people in Phnom Penh, Cambodia. They also thought that far more than a quarter of them were for international products.

Those numbers may surprise you; they may also mean nothing to you. But here in the U.S. young people see between three and five thousand ads per day, a number that's been gradually on the increase since the ad industry started just over a hundred years ago. And most of the products advertised are made by U.S. companies.

In 2008, Cambodian youth had very quickly begun to catch up to American youth in terms of daily ad views. The economy of the country hadn't caught up yet, however, and a large percentage of those ads were for non-local products. Perhaps most significant, none of the media literacy or advertising criticism that emerged over the last century in the U.S. were given time or space to develop in Cambodia. Far more frequently than in the States, young people didn't even identify the messages as advertising. And the ads had been proven to work.

Yet advertising was making people feel a part of global culture. So even as it failed to improve the national economy, upbraided young women who didn't conform to an ideal not always so different from the one outlined in the *Chbap Srei*, promoted a lifestyle of sexualization and substance abuse unthinkable to the traditional elder generation, and repeated slogans with a regularity unseen in the country since the Khmer Rouge, people were excited.

Cambodia was changing.

1

Ryna: It is Also About the War

―――――――――

"I have four siblings," the beautiful and confident Lorn Sosaryna started by telling me. She was different from the other girls. Louder. Happier. More confident. Growing up disaffected in the U.S. made me uncomfortable around such aggressive grace and ease of manner, but I tried to act cool. "Three sisters and one brother," she elaborated.

It is stereotypically Cambodian to introduce oneself with a recitation of one's closest family members, and the hierarchy they created. I had gotten used to it, although I begged off from providing such myself: Describing my estranged relationship to my dysfunctional, alcoholic family did not go over well in a culture that prized familial relationships above all else, nor among teen girls who once asked me to explain *beer*.

"We live with two of our parents, but they do not stay with each other much because they work different places. My father works in Oddar Meanchey province, next to Thai border, and my mom has to work mainly in Siem Reap and Thailand." Ryna's mother and sister ran "an agency," Ryna said, but was unspecific about what the agency did. Likely she did not have the vocabulary to describe it, but it was also possible that she had reasons to remain vague.

Sosaryna—Ryna, the girls called her—was one of the only girls at the Euglossa Dormitory for University Women who had traveled outside of Cambodia. I was trying to interview all the girls before I left the country, but scheduling an hour to chat with someone concurrently pursuing both legal and medical degrees at two universities across town from each other, with perhaps a third course of study at a different school, as many of the young women here were undertaking, made my goal seem unattainable. Ryna had time for me: She was only studying law and international relations. "Is this why you have visited Thailand—with your mother?" I asked.

Ryna flipped her long straight hair back behind her shoulder. She wore a pink polo shirt, because she had already been to school that day, so was no longer required to wear the white button-down blouse and long navy skirt combo that made up university uniforms throughout the country. In the stifling heat of January, the girls seized any excuses for costume changes. They preferred not to acknowledge that they produced sweat, but this was difficult to do when heavy poly-blend fabric clung to their thin bodies, proving for all the world that Cambodian ladies emitted odor and waste like any other animal.

It was oddly reassuring to me, when they sweated. I had slept, eaten, showered, cried, vomited, and you don't want to know what else with these thirty-two young Cambodian women for six weeks and had yet to discover what they did when they menstruated. I had also never seen a razor in the dorm, but attributed this to Cambodians having little to no body hair. At least I did, until the day I walked into my bedroom to find one of my roommates tweezing hairs out of her armpits, one by one. It looked painful.

"It is also because of the war," Ryna responded to my question about travel. "In Cambodia in about 1993, '94, '95, we have civil war and so my parents worry about my education. They have some friends in Thailand who gave us a place to live so I went there to study from kindergarten to primary school."

"What does your father do?" I asked.

"My father, before, he work as government officer but now he is retire and so he has not many things to do. He work with farming. We have some land in the forest."

"Which government was he an officer with?" In her lifetime, there had been the current democratic one; UNTAC; and, before that, the Vietnamese-backed People's Republic of Kampuchea. It was a lot, for 18 years. Many Americans Ryna's age couldn't name all the U.S. presidents they'd lived under.

I was also just curious about her father. He was an incredibly kind and intelligent man, very imposing. He was also the only man I'd met that initiated arguments about politics with young women. I thought he was great.

"Under our Prime Minister Hun Sen," Ryna explained. "He was a soldier." She was hazy on the details.

I switched tracks. "If you didn't live at Euglossa, what do you think you would be doing with your life?" This query was the impetus for the interview series I was conducting. The country was poor, and there were not many opportunities for young women besides working in the garment factories. Most, still, could not afford to go to school. I knew by then very well what life was like for the handful of female students who would receive a higher education, but what about the other four million young women in the country? Ryna knew some of them, and knew how lucky she was.

"I still continue my study and go to university," Ryna mused. "And I will work, maybe helping my mom's company, the agency, or work for other place. If I didn't come to Phnom Penh I might be just a normal girl." She became sad at that word, *normal*. "I have no dream, I have no thoughts, it's just… work, earn money, and have my family. Now because I have the dorm, I study a lot and learn how to have a dream and make a dream come true. So I have a dream and I am now on a process of making my dream come true. And it made my life different because, now I am trying to help my country. Not just my family, which is only six people. I want to help the whole country."

It was a dream she shared with the other young women in the dorm, and they were aware that it would be difficult to achieve. Ryna and her sisters, the first large group of young women to go to college in Cambodia, faced harassment from classmates and faculty just for being in school. They didn't read it as such, refusing to acknowledge the tiny regular barriers consistently placed between them and their dreams, but homework assignments on whether or not girls should be educated at all, comments from fellow students about dropping out to get married and have children, lessons worked into the classroom about women's rightful place in the home and men's place in government—these mounted. They had even begun to affect me.

"Do you think there will be difficulties in achieving your dream?" I asked.

"Sure," Ryna said. "I have a really big dream. I want to be a governor. And governor is just the first step of my dream. The very big dream is being a member of National Assembly. I know that it is really big and dangerous as well, but I have a really good plan. First you have to get a very good and high education, so I am applying for a scholarship in the U.S.

to improve my English. When I come back, I will apply for being the civil servant. I will work very hard, and I think that even if I don't have money to give someone to get a position, my hard working will save me."

By then I was used to the subtle acknowledgement of ubiquitous corruption. *Giving someone money to get a position* was bribery, and the young women in the dorm accepted it as another cobblestone in their career path, because they seemed to have no other choice. "To be a civil servant, we still need some bribery money to give to the higher officer. This has become our culture," Ryna admitted. She wasn't quite sure what to do about it. "I have no thousands, millions of dollars to give to get a position, at which I can earn only like twenty-five dollar or thirty dollar." She remained optimistic. "I think we still have a chance to get a position if we are really good. We have to show them," she said.

I asked Ryna what she meant when she said her dreams were *dangerous*. Futile, maybe. This was a system designed to keep poor young women from decision-making power for the foreseeable future.

"Cambodian politics now, it's dangerous because only one person lead the country for almost thirty years, and I know that they won't give up." She was referring to Hun Sen. He had been in power for twenty-three years by then, and was on his way to becoming the longest-serving prime minister in the history of prime ministers. Even before taking the title, he'd been a member of every ruling party in Cambodia since 1975. "People around him support that person because that person give them too much benefit, but only those people benefit, not the country benefit. But for me, I like trying dangerous things. I like trying things that people say it is difficult to do. And when I get over it? I think, *Oh, I'm so good, I'm special.*" She laughed. "Really, it is what I think. It helps me get over difficult things."

"What if you were, like you said before, just a normal girl?" I asked her.

"A normal girl mean, you have no big dream, just live with your own things. Your community is just your family. I can say that now I am not a normal girl because I have big dreams. Even my friends at school they think a big dream is just earning money. They want to be lawyer. Lawyer is really good looking and can earn a lot of money, but what they do to use all of this money? *I will have my family*, they say to me. *We can buy good cars, we can buy a good house.* All of those things that they say to me are just normal things. They have normal life. I don't have normal life because I want to do something good."

I had also been talking to other women in Cambodia about their dreams. Women Ryna would probably call *normal.* "I met a woman that works in the garment factory yesterday," I told Ryna. I had, and three of her friends, too. They made jeans for American clothing stores you probably shop at. "She told me, *Someday I would like to be a manager at the garment factory but I will never achieve my dream.*"

"Oh, that is the barrier," Ryna explained. "This is a very big obstacle that you have a dream, but you have think that it will never come true."

"Is that part of being a normal girl?" I asked her.

"Yes, it is," she said. Ryna had been born in a Thai border camp in 1986. I knew this because she had drawn a zine about her early life in the camp. Stick figures marked *Thai police* watched over other stick figures marked *Cambodian,* with machine guns. It was the only stable home in her early life; the zine also describes a father constantly on the run and a mother and siblings living in poverty and fear.

The border camps had always been a point of confusion for me. In movies, they were portrayed as reasonably well-organized temporary shelters with plenty of food, water, and legal assistance for all seeking asylum. Yet in the devastation of Cambodia, 1979—and given the historically contentious relationship between Thailand and Cambodia—these spaces seemed unlikely refuges.

When the Khmer Rouge regime fell, people were broken and devastated, but the Vietnamese invasion that ousted Pol Pot and company merely kicked off a civil war that would rage for almost two more decades. Once Cambodians were finally able to walk away from the forced labor and displacement that had guided their lives for four years, many returned home or resettled somewhere new and nearby. The nation of rice farmers quickly realized: There hadn't been enough rice planted in the final days of the failing regime. More would go hungry, and soon.

It was too much for those who had watched neighbors, friends, and family members starve to death. Many left. Picked up and walked to Thailand. Only then did the United Nations High Commissioner for Refugees (UNHCR) step in and establish camps, many within just a few days. The UNHCR also attempted to coordinate food aid in a corrupt nation in the midst of a civil war with no rule of law. Small gestures toward fixing a massive and deeply embedded problem. Those who lived in the camps say the hastily installed system didn't work.

One refugee, now in the U.S., had once told me that life did not improve much in the camp, although getting there had been an enormous challenge. "Even though you're in the camp, it's still—I still had a difficult time to live in that camp," He explained. "The camp is just, like, in the middle of nowhere," he said He had laughed at the preposterousness of it, and I liked his sense of the absurd. He had been at Khao-I-Dang, a camp not too far away from the one Ryna was born in. He described life there as tenuous on good days. "All the food and water is supplied by the UNHCR—you couldn't get it from anywhere. No market, nothing. So each family was given one or two buckets of water per day. If the next day, no truck comes in, it means that you have no water." For him, living in the camp wasn't much of an improvement over his previous life under the *Angkar*.

Ryna, however, would have no such comparison. She didn't remember the camp she grew up in very well, and the picture of how her family had gotten there was also foggy. "Do you know what your family was doing during Khmer Rouge time?" I asked her. "Do you think that time affected your life?"

"I don't think that Khmer Rouge affect to my life," she said, shaking off the notion. She sort of meant, culturally. "At that time, if you have knowledge, if you are university student, if you are professor, you will be brought to be killed." Her family supported her studies. Ryna, like the rest of the girls in the dorm, considered the Khmer Rouge's anti-intellectualism their most unforgivable crime. For this to not sound crass, you may need to keep in mind how much they Just. Loved. Learning. "Some other parents still scared about that period and have problem with education. But my family have no problem with that," she concluded.

As far as she was concerned, the challenges Ryna's family faced started in earnest after they left the refugee camp and returned to Cambodia. "My dad was a soldier at that time and he went to the, I don't know what they call it—the fighting place all the time." This was the ongoing battle for power between the Khmer Rouge and the Vietnamese. "My mom had to stay, only her, with four daughters and so it is quite scary for her and she has like a really big responsibility for the safety of all the girls, and also herself. We have to move from one place to another. Two of my sisters, one she studied to grade three and another got into grade six, and that's it. They have no chance to study anymore. But I and my sister and my brother, we got chance to study."

"Do you remember that time—moving around with your mom?"

Ryna squinted her eyes at the top bunk she sat under. We were in her dorm room, and her roommates were in class. "I remember when I was three years old, I was in a district in Banteay Meanchey province, during UNTAC. They come to help us with the election."

Ryna would have been six when UNTAC started. "I was in kindergarten class," She explained. "I remember one night there was a man came to my house. He told my mother, *You cannot stay at your house tonight because there will be someone come and do something bad.* And so we, my mom and all the daughters, just take everything we can hold and sleep to the house next to our house in our neighborhood. The next day, when we came to our house, everything had been destroyed. Everything was all over the place like someone tried to find us. This is what I see and understand. My mom contact to my dad and my dad want us to move. I don't know the position of my dad at that time, I just know that he is soldier and that he was not at home often, even forget his face.

"At the time, my mom has no money because we were building a house. We were staying in a really small house, I can remember, and we are on the process of building a new house and she take all of her money to that house. We have no money, and we travel by a car. It is really scary and my mom told me not to say anything." She laughed. "We went to the house of our relative in Banteay Meanchey province because my mom has no money. And that man gave us five hundred Riel, which is like twelve dollars, and so we move on by the car. And every step I remember the feeling of scary. My mom told me not to say anything, I stay still. Do not let other people know who you are."

"When we arrive in other place it is like a new village? Which we have land so my mom tried to build a small house by ourselves by helping from other people, other men in the area, and we live in a very small house. My mom, she fried the banana to sell and she asked me to sell by taking it on a tray and put it on my head and just sit on the street. I was small at the time but I feel pity myself, that I should do all of this work because when I stay at my last home we kind of in a very good position. I know that it is a very difficult period for us."

"How long did you sell bananas in the street?" I should admit I was shocked. I had grown comfortable with the idea that the young women I lived with in the dorm, although raised in poverty, weren't raised in *that kind* of poverty. Her voice trembled with the shame of it.

"Quite a long time. Maybe two years? We also have a small farm in the back of our house. My mom grows rice and doing all those things alone. Sometimes she sell things illegally. At that time cigarettes are not allowed to sell and also some sugars, they do not pay tax. So they have to bring it on the back of the bike and travel at night time to the market to sell because at the daytime the police will catch them."

"Where did the illegal goods come from?"

"Probably from Thailand because we were next to Thailand. I don't know much but I know it was a really bad period for us. My dad was a soldier and he had no time to stay with us. I'm not sure of the position of him at that time, but people tried to come and destroy us. And so living in that small area and we have no money and my mom has to do all this work alone and I feel that it is really a hard work. Even the school, we have only one small school, and I went to the school only like two times, and then we move."

Right. Her father was fighting a civil war. Did being reminded of this make me feel like less of an ass for being surprised she sold bananas on the street at six? It did not. "What was it like for you, the fighting?" I asked.

"I remember this one time that I was in school, and there were bombs?" She raised her voice at the end, like a question, like a shy girl, and not one relaying a narrative of combat. She laughed, nervously, and repeated herself. "Bombs. We were starting in the class and then we heard something like *dun dun*—what is it? Even teacher was like, *What is it?* No one know. The sounds come more and more, near us, and so we realized that it is the bomb. So our teacher is like, *Everyone run out of the building because it's nearly come to the school building,* and so we ran out and we ran out and the teacher said *OK roll down!* And we roll down and then, *OK run!* And then we run to home." Her English was so natural she didn't flinch in substituting *like* for *said* when she described her teacher. It was absurd to feel proud of her for this when she was describing how she survived a bombing campaign, but I was proud of that, too.

"I feel so scary and a little bit also fun. I never feel that feeling before. When I was that small maybe I felt some bombs, but I did not know. I was in grade one at the time and I can remember, a feeling of fun as a children but also scary." She giggled. What she was feeling was the excitement of adventure. Physical danger was not open to women but Ryna had tasted it. "I can remember it. The feeling," she said. Wistful.

"Do you remember when the civil war ended?" I asked her.

She shook her head. "We move, and then I went to Thailand. And so when I was in Thailand I knew nothing about it."

We had been talking for hours and it was time for dinner, so I thanked her, and hugged her, and went back to my room. I knew that, as a journalist, there were certain things I should have asked, or asked more forcefully. But I also knew that, in Cambodia, and as a woman, there are certain things one does not ask.

Look, reader: Ryna was beautiful, charming, and confident. Her superior English skills and easy smile made her the darling of every casual visitor to the dorm, and every American dignitary who came by on official business. In later years she would go on to meet Cambodian heads of state, business leaders, Hillary Clinton. She would travel and receive scholarships and post Facebook statuses about typical American teenage things like extremely expensive footwear and boys and hating homework. For all her talk of what normal was in Cambodia, she would soon achieve normal girlhood in the U.S., although neither of us knew it at the time.

Yet I also did not know what side of what war her strong, smart, wonderful father had been on. I'm not sure she ever did either.

The question I asked myself was: Would I love her any less if her father was in the Khmer Rouge?

2

Rewriting the Rules

Be Patient

It was Ryna's idea, originally. *Ryna's*. She was studying the law, and had become interested women's issues. She was not happy with the *Chbap Srei*. So one night we invited all the girls to come in and sit on the tiles of the second-story kitchen floor to discuss. A giant pile of flip-flops outside the door respectfully awaited the end of our talk, whereupon each young woman would quietly bow out of the room backwards. It was not a bow toward me. The act was performed nearly by accident, worked into body posture via muscle memory, each one backing out, bending slightly, looking up smiling as she slipped on one sandal at a time, arched and leaning against the doorframe. Maybe they would be her shoes, maybe not. Her sisters would forgive her if not.

Chbap Srei. Girl Law. Rules for Girls. The dictums had existed for hundreds of years, and Ryna felt they no longer applied.

"What I'm really interested in hearing," I started nervously, looking at Ryna. I rarely got to see all of the residents of Euglossa at the same time. There was so much potential in the room it was unnerving. "Is what kind of rules you think should apply to all girls. Like the *Chbap Srei*? If you could rewrite it, what would it say?"

There was silence in the room. Of course there would be silence in the room.

We had spent six weeks making zines, and within the confines of our three-story haven, had built up a library of around fifty locally produced publications that they consulted when they wanted to know something about each other, or about themselves. The thirty-two primly seated young women I was now towering above in a state of mild agitation had, whether they knew it or not, created a vast archive of documents on their nation's development and progress. They had invented, tested, improved, deepened, and distributed among a small but international audience a dialogue about what young women in a developing country might need. Sure, they came from some of the poorest rural areas in the world, but they now occupied positions of privilege. Ryna, at least, felt it was time to test what they could do with it. I wondered if the rest of them would agree.

"I guess what I mean is, imagine if all girls in the country were able to have what you have, were able to come and live with you here in the dorm, were able to have the kinds of privileges you have. Would you want that? What sorts of things do you think would need to change, in your country, for that to be possible? And what sorts of rules do you think would apply to everyone then?"

It was a difficult task: Pretend that what you have, everyone has, and then invent an imaginary body of policy that assures and strengthens those privileges, codifying them as rights. Yet that was basically what I was asking them to do. It was the only way I could think to open the conversation. Because if I had said, *What do you think should change in Cambodia?* We would have been there for a hundred years.

"If other girl can live like us?" Amoun asked.

"Yes," I said. "What rules might apply, if what you have access to here became normal?"

There was silence again, but a thoughtful one. A long one. Then it broke.

"To be patient," Narin said quietly, her hand on her sister's knee.

"Yes," Ryna and many others murmured assent. "Be patient."

Thus began the process of drafting a new set of rules for Cambodia.

•　　•　　•

Girls Should be Allowed to Choose Marriage Partners by Themselves in Consultation With Their Parents
"What else would you change, if you could?" I asked the room. The termites along the back wall walked a happy trail on the outskirts of our discussion. *You don't even know, termites,* I thought. *Someday when these women are actually in charge, you will look back on all this …*

"That the girl have to ask that their parents—"Amoun was cut off by Sotheary, who finished the thought without hesitating: "Arranged marriage."

"What?" I said. Then I said it again. "What?"

"Arranged marriage," Sotheary repeated.

Her pronunciation of the phrase was flawless, that wasn't the problem. Neither was the issue that I wasn't familiar with the concept. It's just that I'd had hundreds of discussions with these young women on marriage and family life, on their hopes and dreams for the future, and had no idea they didn't always have input into the selection of a husband. I quickly scanned every bit of information I'd accrued over the last six weeks for any previous indication that young women, when they married, were not free to choose their own partners and came up with nothing. I recalculated conversations with these young women, and others around the country: Maly just last week had told me that she felt secure in her decision to put off marriage until 24. She was sure that someone would still want her then, even though it was kind of old. Amoun daydreamed about falling in love with a boy, the perfect boy, the right boy, and made up songs about him in the shower. Another young woman had planned out her wedding, her first child, her second child—the man she married only ever appeared as a mechanical figure, a hazy, imprecise ghost. Not because she couldn't envision him, maybe, but because she may not have much say in the matter. Come to think of it, where these husbands emerged from was never made clear, and it had never occurred to me to ask. Perhaps the pressures on these young women regarding marriage were not limited to the normative social ones I was familiar with growing up. Familial pressures, not just to marry, but to marry someone the family had located, often by contracting the services of a marriage broker or committing other family resources to the cause, were a totally different ballgame.

"Oh. Arranged marriage." I said, feigning coolness after my recalibration. "And what do we think of arranged marriage?"

"That it's not so cool," said Ryna.

"Does anyone like arranged marriages?" I asked. Maybe a little too relieved. The practice held merit. Studies showed arranged marriages tended to last as long, or longer, than marriages between partners who selected each other.

In unison, they all yelled, "No!"

I bet some of their parents liked the practice of arranged marriage just fine. "Does anyone at *all*?" I checked again.

"Yes, but we want to choose our own life," the stunning Jorani said, almost shouting above the others to be heard. Botum, next to her, and just as beautiful, nodded hard. She was the only girl in the dorm with a boyfriend, at least the only one who'd shared her secret with me. I wasn't supposed to tell anyone and at first I thought it was because of the rules of the dorm. Now I understood that it might also be because her parents had invested in a matchmaker. These were both emotional and economic issues at stake.

For the rest of the girls, too, although they preferred to think only about romance. "In my point of view, I think the arrangement of marriage—it must come from my heart and also come from my parents' heart," Chenda added. "Both of us have to agree, in this situation. If I just respect and I love him and my parents doesn't agree, that is not so good, too. I think both of us have to agree."

I scanned the room for agreement. "What does everyone think of that?" I asked.

"Yeah," they said. Their casual English slang made me angry for a second, until I realized I had probably taught it to them.

"You know, we have one story of Tum Teav. Because of arranged marriage, in the end they all die." Chenda was referring to the beloved Romeo-and-Juliet-style tale that had been retold in countless film, book, and bedtime stories.

In it, a monk, Tum, falls in love with a beautiful young woman, Teav, and leaves the monastery for her. Unfortunately, she has been promised to another, a government official—plans that are put on hold when her great beauty is thought to be sufficient to marry the king (or become his concubine, depending on the version). Upon learning of the plan, Tum comes to the palace and professes his love for the girl in song; the king, swayed, declares the two lovebirds must marry. In some versions of the story, Teav's greedy mother again attempts to wed her daughter to the government official. Tum, learning of the plan, secures a decree from the king that he is to be allowed to marry Teav, but stops off at some party and stupidly has a few too many, bragging loudly of his love for Teav without revealing the document. Whereupon the government official's guards fall upon the former monk and beat him to death. (In other versions, the jilted fiancé kills him directly.) Teav finds his body and slashes her own throat in sorrow, or otherwise takes her own life. A popular film version, which includes a sex scene that begins with a closed-mouth kiss and a declaration of undying love and ends with, yes, an axe splitting a log and water being poured on the split, also has Teav's sister dying when Tum is slayed.

The hyper-romance does not end there, although an American film, epic poem, or novel exploring the heights of melodrama might. No, in the popular film version, the royal decree is discovered in Tum's closed, dead fist, which provides just enough foreshadowing to explain the entire wedding party's appearance in the next scene, in great wooden shackles, at the foot of the king. He calls for Teav's family, friends, and fellow villagers to be treated like peasants and then—although I admit I may have missed something here—buries them up to their necks in dirt. Then an iron plow is attached to a water buffalo, and they are decapitated. No kidding. The final scene of the film is a field of bloody heads, the imagined consequences of conspiring to restrain a couple from romantic love.

We had watched it together a few nights previous. "That's preposterous!" I had cried over the credits, straining the girls' vocabulary. They had looked at me blankly, then surmised I might be sad over the events of the film, the deaths of Tum and Teav.

"Do you not think the town deserves punishment for keeping them apart?" Someone asked me.

"By being buried up to their necks and ploughed over, like the land?" I had to retort. "No." I was upset. I'd never actually been upset with them before, only with situations that affected them. I lived in a Cambodian girl utopia. I did not expect the logic of violent bloodshed to become a part of the package. I struggled to read the acceptance of vengeance as their undying belief in romantic love, but I knew it was more than that. I had once been on a bus full of folks heading to Kampot when a dog ran in front of our vehicle and almost got hit. As he scampered away into oncoming traffic, a motorcycle struck him. The driver was fine, but angry; he got off the bike and kicked the dog, who flew up into the air, and flipped over before falling down again. Everyone on the bus laughed. Historians have attributed a certain vindictiveness to Cambodians, connecting the legend of Tum and Teav to the brutalities committed under Pol Pot, and sometimes I could see it. I just didn't want to see it in these young women.

Chenda summarized the group's feelings about arranged marriage. "We have a bad idea of it. When we want to marry someone, this should be agreed both of children and their parents."

"Girls should choose marriage partner... and consult parents?" Kimlong asked the room, testing language to jot on the white board for our own rule book.

Tum and Teav had seemed to make a pretty good case for not allowing authority figures such decision-making powers at all, so I clarified: "Does anyone think you should *not* consult your parents? That you should just decide on your own?"

They weren't going for it. "No, you have to consult them," Leung told me. No question.

"Because they worry for us," Ryna explained.

.   .   .

Girls Should Be Educated in Schools Alongside Boys
"You know," Chenda began. She was extremely articulate, and quickly learning smart-girl gestures, like removing your glasses to better point something out. To gesture emphatically but diplomatically. No accusatory fingers, that sort of thing. She had a full, square face she scrunched into unpleasantness around abstract concepts she found distasteful. "One thing is that many people say, girls should not be independent in school. They should stay at home and get education from their parents," she said. "This point, I—I don't like this and I want to change. Because if we just get education from our parents, I think it is not enough. Maybe we cannot know how wonderful this world. And maybe our world, normally, is not too broad. Maybe if we meet another person, we have nothing to talk with them because of our limited knowledge, I think."

Chenda rested her case.

"Girls should be educated in schools alongside boys," My roommate Lili said. I wrote it down as she spoke. Then we broke for the night.

.   .   .

The Fish Heads Look Amazing

First thing the next morning, I accompanied Botum to the food shop, determined to learn the words for Cambodian spices and vegetables. Which of course meant I brought my tape recorder, because the names for Cambodian foods are really hard to pronounce and remember. Also I am lazy and afraid of the Khmer alphabet. "So today you will make lunch, yes?" I asked her. Botum was not comfortable with English, so everything I posed was slowed down, and formed as a question.

"Yes," she agreed, searching my eyes to make sure we understood each other.

"Do you know what you will buy?"

"I—I don't think I know," she said. Meaning, *I don't know the English words for these things please don't make me try to say them.*

"OK, let us look at the food together." I persevered. She was not doing well in her English class and the dorm manager Ms. Sonrith Channy had asked me to keep an eye out. One of the easiest ways to teach English is by trying to learn the native language. It levels the playing field, and all parties become invested in exploring meaningful communication. We glanced over the low table before us, in the living room of our neighbor. It was just an open front room with vegetables and meats strewn across a table, no refrigeration, no protection from flies. I pointed to things and cracked jokes in English as Botum translated the names of foods into Khmer.

"Oh, the fish heads look amazing!" I exclaimed in exaggerated delight. She laughed.

"I will buy this," she offered, holding up a plant. "For *Tek Reung,*" she said. I repeated it. It was a dish I didn't like very much.

"What do you think about the market today?" I asked. I liked most Khmer foods but the deliberately bitter ones were always prepared whenever one of the girls got a sniffle, and I was tired of hearing about the magical healing properties of sour-tasting sticks. I missed cheese. Real cheese, not *prahok,* the fermented fish paste that sometimes showed up on foods in restaurants that told you they served cheese. Mozzarella. Provolone. Wisconsin cheddar. I missed pasta. I missed leafy green salads. I missed preparing my own food.

"I think it's expensive today. Someday it's more expensive. Today." Botum answered.

The tiny storefront was bustling with women. She was the youngest. "How come there are no men shopping here?" I asked my friend. I sort of knew what I was getting into, but thought her answer might be interesting.

"What?" She asked, genuinely confused.

"How come there are no boys shopping?" I asked her again. "It is only women."

"I don't understand," she said. She searched my eyes again, but deeper, and with slightly more concern.

"Where are the boys?" I asked deliberately. I probably sounded agitated. My question was strange, sure, but not incomprehensible.

"Boys." Botum's eyebrows were knit tightly together.

"How come no boys shop today?" I asked again. Slowly, maybe too loud.

Finally she appeared to understand. And smiled. "I don't know," she said, but couldn't get it out before her mouth broke into wide giggles. These turned into outright laughter, and then distinctly unladylike guffaws.

I laughed too, but wasn't sure what was going on. "Why are you laughing?" I had to ask.

"I'm surprise!" Botum said in a high-pitched voice. She was clutching her stomach, a bag of vegetables in her fist. I had never seen her laugh so hard—had never seen any of the girls laugh so hard, ever. They were usually much more cautious with their volume, their emotions, their public displays. She couldn't help herself. It was too funny.

I stopped laughing. I'd figured out what was going on. "You are surprised that I would think that boys would shop," I said.

"Yeah," she said, her body bent in half, now speaking through a more girly peal of giggles. "Why you say that? It is incredible!"

•   •   •

Women Should Have the Right to Leave the Home and Join in Social Activities as Men Do, Or Be Involved in Politics
By that night, I was probably known behind closed doors as The Girl Who Believed Boys Shopped For Food.

"Should women have as much right to work outside of the home as men?" I asked. There were murmurings of dissent.

"No," someone said then, in a low voice. Others giggled. The part of me educated by feminists was horrified, if also a little bit pleased that they had gotten over their fear of contradicting the foreigner.

Ryna jumped up to admonish the room. "It's not bad for you, that only the men leave the country and only men go to work and you just stay at home?" She looked around, her brash good looks taking center stage while she glared at her sisters, her authority slightly undercut by her cartoon panda pajamas. "Can you *do* that?" She was nearly screeching.

The room broke into laughter.

"Yes," someone said, answering my original question, so addressing me directly. Yes, women should have the right to work outside of the home, as men do. "As much right, yes, also to join in the social activity, and the politics."

Ryna sat down. The room agreed with her. The statement worked in theory, sure, on our clean white board. But I looked around the room and thought about how Botum had never seen a man at the market. Grocery stores, maybe, but those were for foreigners and rich people. The American movies they loved, that might have given them a vision of gender equality, had plenty of scenes of women shopping, cooking, and waiting on men, although none in my memory of men shopping, or waiting on women. An occasional temporary gender reversal in a market-tested, all-ages flick might have a male lead in an apron showing off his prowess in the kitchen, but this was always an act of romance, a one-time chore to prove love.

Having women in society and politics meant men would have to learn to shop. I wondered how long it would be before the idea wasn't funny anymore.

•　　•　　•

Girls Should Be Brave Enough to Make Eye Contact With and Speak to Boys
"What the *Chbap Srei* says is the women, in the past, cannot look at the boy by eye contact. Like if you are a boy, and I see you, I must go like this, and look down." Maly bowed her head in demonstration, promptly losing her

train of thought as she caught one of the girls teasing her. Maly didn't often play-act. She was planning on becoming a bank manager.

"That seems very difficult," I said. Of course most upper-level bank jobs are held by men, and most of her customers would be whoever controls the family money—also men. How would she do her job?

"Yeah, and cannot talk to you," she added. To not be able to look at or speak to her customers or colleagues would be totally disastrous for Maly's future career. "We need to do wiley communication," she said.

"Wiley communication?" I had no idea what that might be.

"Yes. We have to communicate by another way."

I noticed with some distress that she had started using the past tense but ended up using the present. It wasn't the *Chbap Srei* themselves, nor that these young women could recite them so clearly, that nagged at me. They didn't acknowledge that these rules had an impact on their behavior. "Hm," I said aloud. "So, girls should make eye contact with, and speak to boys? Is that a fair way of stating a new rule?"

"Women, girl, should be brave enough to make eye contact, to make communication. Yes."

"Sure. That makes sense," I said. "I want to point out that it would be a lot easier to have a say in who your marriage partner would be if you could make eye contact with and speak to boys, right?"

"Yes." They all agreed. They did see a logic to it.

•   •   •

Women Should Hold Positions of Power in High Society And in Politics
"What about women in politics?" I asked. Television coverage of various political gatherings pictured impressively monotonous groups of men discussing the state of the nation.

"They cannot sit at the high positions," Chenda said disparagingly. She scowled at this.

"Is there a law in Cambodia right now that says that is not possible?" Who knew? Maybe there was. There are laws in the U.S. that state you can't give a donkey a bath.

"No," came the response from our law students, drawn out a bit as they considered the implications.

"So the reason women do not hold high political office might be because they are not trying to hold a high political office?"

"Yes," said Amoun. She was confident this would change in her lifetime. There were female politicians already—district governors, parliament members. Not many, but Amoun perked up when they came on the TV or appeared in the papers.

I liked her confidence, but studies back home regularly showed that female candidates running for political office were just as ambitious as male candidates, although still received less funding, fewer endorsements, and a lower level of media support. Empowerment, in other words, was no solution.

"What if we made it a rule that women *should* hold high political office?"

"Oh, that is a good idea," Amoun concurred immediately.

"Yes," Ryna added. "I like it, very much."

We broke for bed and homework.

·   ·   ·

You Are Very Clever

I was trying to keep up with my Khmer lessons during the day. Not only was it fascinating and challenging, but it was teaching me core lessons about Khmer culture. I knew, for example, that there was an entirely different vocabulary for women than for men, but the language was more complex than even that indicated. There were words unique to orders of beings: different words for the same activities applied to monks, kings, or dogs, depending. While the feminine vocabulary did have negatives, I was not really taught what they were. In fact, it was not advised that I learn how to deny anyone anything. I was taught instead how to convey *no* by saying *yes*. My head spun. Not to mention that the written version of Khmer contained thirty-three consonants, twenty-three vowels, and twelve independent vowels. And that there were two separate ways of making letters—a formal and an informal version, similar to cursive and Roman letters, in theory, except that I could neither identify nor distinguish any particular characters in either script. I could barely choose Khmer letters from a lineup of Southeast Asian words. I didn't know what independent vowels were; my instructor wouldn't even let me open a Khmer-language textbook. I was having enough trouble reading situations without trying to add written words to it, too.

And any progress I made seemed to dissipate quickly. As it was explained to me, there are several words in the Khmer language that mean absolutely nothing, but without which a sentence will not be understood. What was also tricky is that even though I had pieced together several ways of saying certain things—*Hello, Come have a cup of coffee with me; The baby duck eats lunch; The monk prefers orange just like me*—there are much better ways of saying them. And so even when I could manage a comprehensible sentence, which was rare, it was usually corrected.

Then, on my very best days, I could say something quite clearly. Make a statement of fact, or pronounce my intentions to go to the store, or communicate something, anything, in Khmer, and the response was always the same. Not a response in kind, a furthering of the communication, a momentary relaxation of the knowledge that I am a foreigner and would never ever understand anything. Instead: a laugh, a cheer, a *Congratulations. Your pronunciation is very good. You are very clever.* But always in English.

•   •   •

Women Should Be Brave, Smart, and Confident, and Should Build and Strengthen Their Abilities
"Women should be brave, smart, and have confident themselves." Botum started off our next session with a clearly thought-out rule. She had been rolling it around in her head all day, probably with the same tenacity with which I had tackled my Khmer lesson that morning.

"Brave… confident…" I wrote it on the board.

"Smart."

"Smart," I repeated.

"Smart. And confident," Botum added. "And one thing: Should be build their ability."

"Should what?" I asked for clarification.

"Should build their ability, yes, by themself." I wrote it down.

• • •

Women Should Learn to Protect Themselves
"What about, *Women should work to gain physical strength*," I suggested.
There was no agreement.

"Ohh," some said. "Mhmm," went others.

"Meaning?" Chenda asked. She was skeptical.

"Meaning," I said, "if a tiger attacks you…" This was an example
I used a lot in the U.S. *If a tiger attacks you*, I liked to ask groups of young
people,… *is it really going to matter which brand of shoes you are wearing?* Or
maybe,… *do you think having a fancy cell phone is going to help?*

"You must be physically strong," Chenda finished my thought.

"Yes," I nodded. "Then, if a tiger attacks you, you can fight it off or
run away, really fast."

"No…" Lili said.

"Women don't have power as men, but they ask man to solve
solution," Ryna suggested.

"But what if a tiger attacks you?" I asked, pushing my metaphor. I
thought it was a good one.

"If a tiger attack?" Lili repeated pendatically. Then she told me
about a tiger attack just outside of Phnom Penh six months previous. An old
woman had been mauled, and killed, by a tiger, within walking distance of
where we stood. Lili had to tell me to close my mouth, which had dropped
open. My metaphors here sucked.

"We can find a peace solution by…" Ryna started. The girls
laughed.

"Running away," one called out.

"Yes." Ryna agreed.

Botum added, "If a tiger fights girl, you have to take all men and
put in front of the tiger and then you run away." The room broke into waves
of giggles.

Ugh, I was not going to let this go. I really wanted them, in these
couple moments at least, to imagine a solution that did not rely on a male
savior. "What if there were only girls?" I asked. I will also admit that, now

that there was a real danger of tigers attacking my little sisters, I needed to make sure they had a plan.

"We can find a peace way. To discuss with the tiger." Chenda offered. Everyone laughed.

They were really in a mood now. Punchy.

"Oh, you would have a discussion with the tiger? Good plan." I was sort of teasing, but liked that they would not panic. "I think that's perfectly reasonable."

"Actually," Ryna pointed out, "The tiger cannot speak." She said this directly to me. She felt she needed to explain it, as I had recently revealed myself to be someone who thinks tiger attacks exist only as metaphors. My knowledge of the animal's true ability was obviously suspect in her mind. This would probably go down on my permanent record, next to *Someone who believes boys shop for food.*

"We must shout out to call some strong men to help," Chenda suggested.

I nearly spat: "Why would you need a strong man to help you? You are a strong woman."

"We are not as strong as them," Chenda countered.

"We strong in mental, and we strong in heart, but—" Botum began, but lost the vocabulary to explain.

I was becoming desperate. I was half convinced a tiger attack was imminent at which point the largest group of young women in the history of Cambodia to achieve a higher education would be eaten alive because we couldn't settle on a plan. "What about," I stuttered, "what about, is there some kind of, like… maybe the rule should be, *all women carry a rope with them so if a tiger attacks they can set a trap*. And then—pull the tiger up into a tree?"

"Being a girl you cannot do like that," Chenda said. Ironically, she was probably the strongest of them, physically and mentally. It was frustrating to hear her speak of her abilities in such limited terms.

"But it might be easier to carry a rope with you than to have a man around at all times," I suggested. I did not mention that a rope was less likely than a man to have been trained that women were expendable.

She was getting equally angry with me. "No. As you said, we can take something with us to protect ourselves. We are the weak sex. We have to be physical but we have to have, like, a strong mental and a strong heart so we can solve this problem by taking something with us."

"I like that. So, women should protect themselves," I surmised, emphasizing the last word.

"Yes." Chenda, Ryna—even Amoun nodded, my roommate, who flirted her way out of chores.

"Does anyone disagree?" I asked.

"No. We agree."

•   •   •

Young Women and Men Should Have Access to Free High Quality University Education and Housing in their Own Province
"How about educate the student?" Jorani asked. I prepared to write it on the board.

"Should education be free?" I asked. I no longer needed to prompt them. Like most people who find their voice, these young women had figured out that they could say anything they wanted, and even if malformed it was likely to be improved through discussion. How powerful was it, to start rewriting the world the way you wanted it to be?

"Yes. Free general education for student across the area."

Ryna was skeptical, which was an indication that things were about to get interesting. "For free? So where can the government get the money and pay for all the teacher or—" Ryna's head spun with the implications. Maly, next to her, looked concerned. Her sense of economics was bewildered.

"There are many countries that offer free education," Amoun said firmly, although in sweetvoice.

"Yes," a voice agreed in Khmenglish. Chenda's. She planned to teach someday.

"They have figured out how to pay for it, and they are countries that are much bigger than Cambodia, so it is possible." Amoun again. She pushed her long straight black hair behind her shoulder. She was wearing light blue pajamas that alternated kittens with hearts, and said, *My love for you I give you god life! You like to have good life for love!* Kindly nonsense. I had a matching pair in purple.

"Possible, *possible* in the other countries, but—" Cambodian exceptionalism snuck in, the opposite of American exceptionalism. Whereas the recent birth of our nation allows us to presume that our foundations, desires, and ideals mark us better and more authentic and with a higher consciousness than people from other lands, Cambodia was forged at the hands of poverty, a Buddhism tinged with Hinduism, colonialism, the Khmer Rouge and, it must be said, forces under the sway of American exceptionalism over the course of twelve hundred years. Cambodians had come to the exact opposite set of presumptions about their national identity. Their people would always be corrupt, always be poor, always be behind. The international products advertised every day only proved it.

"Every, every country can be the same. Every." Jorani suggested.

"We should think about the quality not just the quantity," Maly added.   "I mean, for education. The quality of student that one day graduate from their university."

"So, free high quality education?" I summed up.

"And place," someone added. Of course they would be concerned about housing. They were the first to see it as a right, since they were given it as a privilege.

"… and housing for students?" I added as I wrote on the white board.

"Yes." Maly agreed. "Have dormitory for the student that come study."

Chenda considered. She wanted to teach young women in the village she came from, because she knew how badly they needed resources. "In home province," she added. Everyone agreed.

•   •   •

Women and Men Should Have Access to a True Democracy and Human Rights
"I want all over the world have democracy and human rights. Not just in the U.S. or in Cambodia, but around the world," Jorani said.

"We need that, we are building it now," Ryna responded. Then something occurred to her. "Anne, can I ask you a question?"

"Yes, of course," I said. This was often the opening query to something amazing. Once a conversation about underpants, another time the history of the U.S. cultural underground, and recently a spirited debate about the merits of cheese that remained a point of contention between myself and

Amoun. She called it *baby food*, and my retort about *prahok* hadn't gone over very well.

"If all countries in the world have democracy, I want to know about, if it becomes a problem?"

Wow. Democracy. How could I explain the difference between how democracies worked on the ground—as the free market—with how they were sold—as freedom of speech? "I think that's a good question," I started. "The way that democracy should work is that everyone should have a voice. But unfortunately what happens right now in the world is that people claim to have a democracy when they do not. Even though in the United States, we claim we have a democracy, actually there are many people we never hear from. Does that make sense?"

"Not really." Chenda scowled at me. She liked precision.

"Well, in a true democracy, people get to weigh in directly on how the government works, and what the rules are, and what the punishments for breaking the rules are. We don't have that in the United States, so it's hard for me to imagine having it all over the world." Brecht once wrote that if the punishment for saying something negative about Germany was too severe under National Socialism, that the same things could usually be said about Austria, without fear of retribution. I wasn't about to criticize Cambodia's particular version of democracy—I could leave any time I wanted and wouldn't have to suffer the consequences. Anyway, as regards imprecise applications of democracy, I could say many of the same things about the United States, without fear of retribution. "If everyone in the world had a true democracy, people would struggle with each other, sure. And they would fight. A lot. However the idea is that no one person or company would have so much power that other people no longer had a say. Right now what we have in the U.S. are big companies that keep some people from being heard. I don't think it is a true democracy," I said. I didn't mention that those companies were some of the same ones that manufactured and advertised goods in Cambodia.

"True democracy," someone repeated.

"You need a true thing," Chenda agreed.

"We need the true thing," Ryna summarized. "Not just the word. True democracy and human rights."

So we added that to the list of rules, too.

3

JORANI: THE COMMUNISTS WON

"My parents encouraged me a lot in study," Jorani started, looking earnest and wide-eyed as she launched into the story of her life so far. She had such perfect features, it hurt to look at her. Like a Disney princess in real life. "Not only in high school but also in university. It is not really possible for a girl—a Cambodian girl—to get higher education, but I am lucky so I can continue my study in Phnom Penh, which is where the university is located. Universities are not located in the provinces—I mean not many, just a few— and the quality is still under consideration."

The uniquely feminine-Cambodian construction of her last sentence struck me. A young woman back in Chicago would have had no problem telling me her university *sucked*—even if it didn't. And compared to Jorani's, it wouldn't have. Once when I visited her at school the English professor pulled me aside to have me translate some first-grade vocabulary words into Khmer. I didn't understand how he could have gotten through a lesson at the college level without them, nor how he had gotten the job in the first place. "What would you be doing with your life if you did not go to school?" I asked her.

"My dream is always to go to university. I committed myself in high school to get a scholarship and study in Phnom Penh, so I study very hard and as a result I got scholarship to both public and private school." She was pursuing law and international relations majors when she wasn't sitting around chatting with me. She put in long, long hours for a 17-year-old.

"Did you ever consider what you would do if you did not..." I started, but she cut me off and tossed her hair behind her shoulder.

"No, because I afraid. I mean, I like study. So I wanted to go to school, I don't want to work. My parents were not higher educated persons, so they work very hard. Anyway I admire them. They sell food in a market in my home province. They make Chinese noodles. I like helping them but I don't want that career for my future job."

Message received: Don't ask what life would be like for Jorani if she hadn't lucked into college—for her a combination of good grades, a teacher who recommended her to Euglossa, willing parents, and the smarts to locate, pursue, and be granted two scholarships. "What are you going to do when you graduate?"

"After B.A., I want to pursue my study in a Master Degree in international relations. Then, make a plan to get into the work as a government official." They would eat her alive in the government. Ryna might prove a match for the entrenched corruption, gender bias, and sexual harassment that were so the norm they were rarely even named, but Jorani was *sweet*.

I worried for her. "Do you have concerns about working in the government?"

"Yes. We just talk about it, the corruption, in my class this morning. My professor told us, the students, that the corruption is big and many people—many high-ranking people are not very educated but they got the certificate, the Ph.D., without going to school. They got it by money."

The news that week had featured stories about a number of high-ranking government officials who held forged degrees. It was met with yawns from the journalists I knew, but students were understandably upset. As far as I was concerned, it explained a lot about, for example, why Jorani's English professor hadn't known basic vocabulary words. "What do you think about a government where people have diplomas and certificates that they did not earn, when you are working so hard to earn your own?"

"Um, I think that they are very smart. They can make a short cut," Jorani said. I adored Jorani, but it is important to underscore that, when faced—even in her imagination—with someone who was essentially cheating her government out of intelligent leaders and her out of a job, she expressed only admiration. It was another uniquely Cambodian attribute, to locate the good within the corrupt. Hopeful and bright-eyed, totally undaunted: Actually she'd probably be fine in government after all. "Anyways, if we compare two person, one they buy and one they study? We can see the quality of them, the work they do, and it is not possible for one to be a diploma without study the law, any law at all, and it will be embarrassment or humiliate themselves. Also our country."

"When you become powerful in Cambodia, what do you want to do with that power?" I asked her.

"The first change I want to make is with education. I think people must be educated to get their dignity. We can lead people but if we lead educated people it will be easier."

This was not only a response to the obvious query, *How will you respond to government leaders forging documents?* It was also a reference to the intellectual purge under the Khmer Rouge had undertaken. "Do you know what your parents were doing during the Pol Pot time?" I'd never asked her before.

"Oh yes. They told me. They were ordered to work hard and just eat a little bit, a small ration, of rice? And they told me that one of their friends died because of eating in a hurried way because she stole something to eat when the guard did not know and she ate very fast. So she become cannot breathe and die. I feel very shock at it. My uncle was blind because of the Pol Pot put something in his eyes. My mom told me something that is hot, but I don't know." Acid attacks have always been common in Cambodia, but a boiling liquid seemed likely, too.

The relationship between education, girls' rights, and the history of mass killing in Cambodia was complicated; it became even more so when you added in American business interests. The young women in the dorm were taught that the way to contend with their country's troubled past was by achieving higher education; that graduating college, as a woman, would heal the nation faster than anything else. People like Nicholas Kristof, a columnist at the New York *Times*, were popularizing girls' education as a way of inspiring social change. Unfortunately, Kristof also tended to believe a woman's place was in the free market; his column would eventually call for an increase in the number of garment factories. His argument was that this would create more jobs, but at current rates of pay—less than half of a living wage, or what it took to survive on in the country—it would also keep more women in poverty, which is why families tended to deny young women the chance to go to school: They simply couldn't afford to have anyone physically capable not contributing to the family income. This was why local NGO workers and journalists tended to roll their eyes when they heard Kristof's name. Yet in the dorm, and in the wider movement for girls' education in Cambodia, he was revered. Mostly for acknowledging that young women in developing nations even existed.

I asked Jorani if she thought her parents' experiences under the Khmer Rouge had an impact on how she grew up.

"I think so, because the ideology of the leader can affect what they're thinking and their way to us…" she paused. "I think if they did not live in the Pol Pot regime, I would be treated more better," she said. Then she surprised me. "Sometimes they say something like *the communists won*, and do not let us express our opinion."

I wasn't sure what that meant. "Jorani, when you were growing up, did you not feel free to express your opinion?"

"I am now feel free to express my opinion," she said, "and that feelings become more and more freer and freer when I come to this dormitory, yes." That freedom was relative, I knew. Restrictions existed on what she could say in school or in public about, say, the prime minister. But increasing admiration for folks like Kristof meant she also had to tread carefully on major women's human rights questions that might come up when looking at, say, the garment trade. *American clothing companies that manufacture in Cambodia like The Gap should double the minimum wage for garment workers*, for example, would be challenged as unsupportive of American business interests, and Kristof would be quoted to keep such a statement from being repeated. It was another way of squelching dissent, and the girls in the dorm were just beginning to perceive it. "But I cannot always express my feeling," she concluded.

On a larger scale, the same pro-globalization sentiments were showing up around the city. "You know, Jorani, since I have been here in Cambodia, one of the biggest changes is…"

"The Gold 42 towers?" She beamed, proud of the skyscrapers the city planned to build. Construction had not yet been abandoned, but soon it would slow, significantly. She wasn't referring to the building itself, however. She meant the idea of economic development it symbolized.

"That's part of it," I agreed. "Also the KFC—Kentucky Fried Chicken—and people dressing more sexy on the street."

"Oh yes," she said, smiling. "Lots of things change every day, every minute. So many things change in Cambodia and also the development increase, the investment also increase, and the aid from many countries. Also, Korea movie. Not just the movie, but also their culture affect to Cambodia. Their dress, their thinking, their hair style, anything. So Korea came to Cambodia with their culture? It's good to learn something new, like the cultural exchange and also the study tour or students that come to Cambodia to learn from each other. That is something good, experience we can learn from them." Jorani and some of her sisters were big fans of Korean films with strong female leads who didn't take any guff. Yet Jorani was among the first to question why an American fast-food company wanted to open an outlet in her homeland.

"It sounds like you think there are bad things about foreign cultures coming to Cambodia, too," I said.

"Well, like, their hairstyle? And the red color… anything, like, any colors of hair and short skirts or something like that, that are opposite to my culture. We should not adopt that." A few weeks ago, Jorani had asked me to define the difference between *Playboy* and punk rock, because one of the girls owned a T-shirt with a punked-out version of the Playboy Bunny on it, with the caption, Punkboy. It had launched a nuanced discussion of fashion, aesthetics, porn, publishing, women's rights, and global media. I could see she'd been thinking over how she wanted her country to reflect and be reflected in each of those arenas. Her concerns about globalization were evident. "Cambodia is a developing country and more investment can be good. But only Cambodian will love Cambodia," she said, and paused to think.

"Yeah, I want to say like that. Only Cambodian will love Cambodia," she concluded.

4

CHBAP SREI TMEIN

Women Should Have Access to Free, High-Quality Feminine Protection
Every night, in a small termite-infested kitchen, I gathered with thirty-two Cambodian women half my age and cracked jokes about human rights. They laughed politely, loving me for trying, too invested in what we were doing to let me derail the process of rewriting the *Chbap Srei*. "What about—" I asked them one night, "and this is a very important issue—what about free cake?"

"No!" They screamed, laughing but angry. "It would make girls fat so we have to find another idea."

Small pontifications on size acceptance and healthy body image fell on deaf ears when poverty and starvation were still daily concerns for their families. I gave up. "OK. How about—there is a rule that someone suggested to me in the United States."

Ryna narrowed her eyes at me. "What is it?" She was suspicious now.

"Do you know how women all menstruate?" There was silence. Yes, they knew it, in theory. Admitting it would not be wise. We were all women, but still, there are some things women did not have to say in Cambodia, even in private. Fine. "And you know that they all have to buy tampons?"

"Tampons? What's that?" Amoun asked.

Oh right. I wasn't sure they knew. I had never seen any of them use, purchase, or be in the same room as menstrual products. They were available for sale at the market, but I hadn't seen any at the dorm I didn't bring in myself.

"Sanitary napkins? Things to protect your underpants when you are bleeding," I explained. They sounded frivolous, although menstruation in traditional Cambodian culture was not. The practice of *Chol Mlop,* a period of isolation from society and instruction in domestic labor occurred at the first period and marked a young woman's preparation for adulthood— although this usually just meant *marriage.*

"Oh." Everyone said. Or: *Yes.*

"So one rule in the United States that was suggested is that all menstrual products be free."

"Oh, really?" They squeaked. Embarrassment turned immediately into joy. If menstrual products were free, none of them would ever have to mention them to store clerks, or ask husbands, sisters, brothers, neighbors to pick them up. They wouldn't have to discuss them at all. They thought it was a great plan.

"Really?" Ryna giggled openly, smiling wide and flashing teeth.

"So we do not have to waste our money," I explained.

"Oh, wow," she said. "Is just suggest, or is the real thing in United States?"

"It is just a suggestion. It is not real yet. Not in the United States, and not anywhere else I know." God, I wished. If menstrual products were federally funded I'd pay my taxes early every year. "What do you think?

"Acceptable!" Leung exclaimed. Her round face, usually so ready to chide, smiled widely.

Everyone laughed. "Free is OK with you?" I asked. The idea that they might have power, someday, to implement such ideas was intoxicating. "I like free too. It's my favorite price."

Then Ryna started thinking critically: "Yes, but we need the quality, and so the free thing I think it's not good in quality but quantity."

I saw her point. "What if they were highest quality and free?"

"Of *course.*" This passed Ryna's muster. "It's the best."

"Anybody else want to say anything?" I looked around the room. "Does anybody want to pay for feminine products?"

"No, not at all," someone in the back said. Even our most staunch business advocates did not see a need to profit from women's reproductive health. "If they are free and high-quality."

"But..." Botum said. She was sitting off to my right, against the wall. There was a gecko scurrying above her, waiting in anticipation for her next thought. "We still feel like..." She trailed off, glancing over at Jorani. She placed her hand on her sister's knee. Jorani finished for her: "Shy."

"Shy?" I repeated.

"Not shy," Jorani explained. "But that it couldn't be like that. That our government think about that, to do something like that?" She could not believe they would ever offer small ways to make women's lives easier.

Botum had become noticeably quiet. She looked frightened. I could be wrong, but I suspected she might be scared about how much work it would take to create an environment she felt was just. Her fear and the relief and laughter over a tiny solution that was so easy to say but would be impossible to argue and never come to pass sat heavily in the room. It had started as a joke but until that moment I don't think any of us realized what it would take to create a world in which we all felt comfortable, and valued, and free.

And I suddenly never wanted anything so bad in my whole life.

·   ·   ·

Women and Men Should Be Granted Free Visas and Open Borders
"So, if free cake is really off the table—" I looked around. They were not finding this very funny, but this rarely stopped me. "—What else do we think would make a good rule?"

"If we can have free visa," someone said immediately.

"For traveling?" Credit cards had not yet entered the mainstream, here. Actually, banks had not really entered the mainstream. I don't think any of their families had accounts with them, including Maly's: her mother was the village money-lender. Most still kept what money they had in gold or cash hidden under the mattress or worn as jewelry. This probably seemed much safer than letting someone in a suit behind bulletproof glass hold on to it for you, even if they gave you a piece of paper in return that promised you could have the money back when you wanted it.

"Yes, to travel," Narin clarified. She was very patient with me. "Because we can go abroad with, like, less pay."

"Open the border," a voice translated from the back of the room.

Something clicked. They wanted the freedom to travel, yes, but what they wanted to avoid paying were the enormous, frequent, and rising costs of bribes. "Less pay," didn't mean lower visa application costs or ticket prices. It meant, fewer people demanding cash with impunity at every step they took toward seeing what the rest of the world might be like.

It would prove a particular challenge for young women, who under the presiding mixture of protectionism, ownership, desire, and concern upheld by traditional notions like those indicated in the *Chbap Srei* were likely to be punished more severely for wanting to venture into the world. Bribes would be harder on women than a consistent fee structure would be. Corruption privatized the control individual men could exert over women's movements.

"Women should be granted free visas and open borders," Narin stated officiously, and I started to write it on the board. "Wait!" She stopped me. "Women *and men* should be granted free visas and open borders."

She was right, we all saw. So I wrote that down instead.

Suddenly

Just like that, we weren't any longer engaged in a process of just thinking about liberating ourselves, as women—we were striving toward basic liberation without concern for gender. A condition of human rights. It happened without planning, without articulation. And it only became clear after a few small moments of resistance, their gently worded corrections to my presumptions about what their futures might be like.

"In many way, we have the gender equality already," Narin told me once. "We have no human right, man or woman. We know that when we get human right" —she pronounced it like this: Human *riee*—"the man will have it faster and better than the woman. But right now, we have none. So."

She had been explaining something else to me, something about food, probably. This was merely an aside. Yet it made sense. Gender equality would be great, she was saying, but so would survival. And survival to her meant the assurance of human rights.

I got it, but was in something of an awkward position. Cambodia was a signatory to the Universal Declaration of Human Rights, a document drafted in 1948 with United Nations delegates from France, China, Canada, and Lebanon under Eleanor Roosevelt. Cambodia signed it in 1992. The U.S. never did.

•   •   •

Dear Everyone Who Want to Be Friends With Me
I became ill. This was a nearly weekly occurrence due to my dedication to food adventuring which meant pretending I had no food allergies at all. (In fact I did, to eggs and peanuts, which found their way into most dishes in Khmer food, so in many ways every meal was an adventure of some kind, although more often a toilet adventure than a food adventure.) I also ate things I bought on the street without even inquiring what they might be, in English or in Khmer. *I have a problem with my stomach*, was the Khmenglish phrase for illness, and it was true: My stomach and I had ideological disagreements over how I should live my life.

I become extremely sensitive when I get sick. Emotionally. Normally I'm fairly daft, although the girls are kind to call it *flexible*, and I tend to overlook or fail to notice things that might make a girl of standard proclivities freak out. When I became sick, however, I noticed, for example, that the entire kitchen always smelled like dried fish, which is a difficult to describe smell like regular fish but more insidious and deeper and sour. Also that termites really ran the show around here. Even in a brand new building, in a safe and clean environment, bugs had forged entire winding paths through the bathrooms and crowded around dropped food in great huddled masses and walked on me when I slept, even in this privileged, educated environment and I cannot tell you how disgusted I was. Finally it was hot. So hot.

The termites normally didn't bother me, but something about their movements and how many of them I imagined there might be if gathered in one room together and how that would look, to see them all moving in a mass like that. My stomach churned. I had met a man a few days beforehand who had wanted to reform the educational system in his village. To initiate this project he installed new concrete floors in the school. Because this has always sounded to me like a scoffable budget item, new floors, in a country where indoor plumbing was still rare, I asked him how that helped. *The termites*, he told me. *They do not crawl everywhere and they do not distract the students.* While sick, I was starting to see how that would help the situation, if only for a little while.

Even away from the kitchen, the smell at the dorm could be atrocious; thirty-two unwashed girls in tropical heat sleeping in tight conditions with no way of cleaning their assorteds except difficult physical labor that takes time they don't have—let's not pretend at the end of the day that anyone was really in the mood to worry too much about their general smell. Not to mention the stink of the city. On less hot days certain neighborhoods smelled of frangipani and bougainvillea, flowers so exotic I couldn't pronounce them and didn't usually try, but this luxury was only for the touristy parts of Phnom Penh and we lived in the rough-and-tumble area, where *no dumping* signs were decorated with piles of garbage and the nearby brown-water open-sewage creek—mis-colored blue in the maps it did appear on, although more frequently it was left off entirely for fear, perhaps, that someone would wish to inner tube down it or drop a line for fish. To call this reek unimaginable is to assume you have never experienced the smells of your own body and to disavow the experiences of millions of people the world over who live in extreme poverty, who live with smells like this every day. Let us instead call it intense.

This was the base perfume of the city, a stench of rotting human waste and animal remains. Over it, in my dorm at least, were laid the smells of thirty-two active women from the countryside, rampant hula hoopers and eager apsara dancers, too busy to wash, trapped in small rooms together for extended study periods in hot, hot weather. Dust is rotten skin, and its smell was a relief from the rest: smells of cooking eggs and blood from fresh cuts of meat, motor oil mixed with gasoline.

The soundtrack was less natural. People hawking cell phone cards to grating pop music. Children laughing. Outsized SUVs blaring along while men greeted each other loudly in congratulations, probably just for being men, I didn't know. Karaoke videos blaring, always, loudly, in the background.

I turned on the TV for comfort and escape. Thinking about the termites and my stupid food mistakes and being so far away from home made me sad, and when I got sad I wanted to watch *CSI*. I hated *CSI* otherwise: It is insipid. All bright colors and sexy people with no critical or engaging elements, just a prettied-up fake crime to pretend to solve with cool gadgets. The world it presents is all high-definition and the music is all blaring guitar and dramatic drum intros and the answer is always waiting to be found. It was all a lie, and it reminded me of the U.S. like nothing else. It was weird, but comforting.

Of course, the thing I wanted to comfort me was not available. There was no *CSI* in Cambodia and for a minute I thought of it as a failure of global media. The basic structure of world peace we were currently building toward—if it did not rely on *CSI* what could it rely on? I became despondent.

Then I found the channel for music videos where you could SMS in your messages, straight to the screen. Sponsored by Heng Meas, *Golden Bird*, recording company, a division of M Entertainment, frequent ads reminded me. I giggled at the messages for hours, until I felt better:

> *All who want be friends to me!*
> *Hello TV people!*
> *Ha ha love to you!*
> *I look for you but do not find, sms to me!*
> *All bright, all friendly: dear world, I love you.*

Etc., etc., etc. It was no *CSI*, certainly. It was one hundred gazillion times better.

•   •   •

Women and Men Should be Given Free Healthcare and Preventative Health Education

Illness would not keep me from our project. I had no choice. "Anne." They started, very serious, when I wandered in cautiously to make some tea. I was visiting the toilet every eight minutes then and wrongly assumed they would take a night off given my condition. They didn't. They were gathered, ready to discuss. I feared some kind of attack if I tried to leave.

"Everyone need the free health care, especially for the poor people. Here in Cambodia, in hospital, like the nurse are—the doctor here—especially in the public hospital, they are very, very mean. They have the corruption, or make it so we have to pay first in order to treat the people."

Oh yes. I was such an easy sell on health care issues right then. I would stay.

"Not just the health care, should be health education too," Chenda added.

"Wow, that's very smart. OK." I wrote it down on the white board. "But I have a question for those of you who are actually going to be working in health care. Would it be OK for you if people did not have to pay for it?"

"It's not OK," my med-school roommate said, quietly but firmly.

Ryna argued with her: "But you can get the money from government—" She stammered in English, then rapid-fired in Khmer for a little while. Impassioned. She took a breath and returned to English. "You will agree to take your money from the government instead of the people?" She accused. Like a lawyer in a courtroom.

"Yes. OK." My roommate looked scared.

In the states we would call it socialized healthcare. Some would argue it was a short step from that to a total communist system of health care, but the communist system of health care in Cambodia was pretty easy to avoid. After the health professionals had been killed off in the mid 1970s, people were selected, largely at random, to create medications with twigs, rabbit dung, mud, and leaves. Those who did have medical knowledge were in the most awkward of positions. They could not offer real care for fear of being discovered.

•   •   •

In Exchange for Health Care and Education All Residents Must Provide a Period of Free Labor for Cambodia

"It is so much free," Amoun said. "Who will pay?"

"The government!" Ryna snapped at her, ready to assure it would happen.

I thought I could see where this was going: The debate over resources. "If the government is going to give you free, high-quality feminine protection, free health care, free preventative health education, high-quality public education, and housing while you're in school, what would you give in return?"

"Give in return to us from them, to the government?" Amoun clarified.

Botum thought about it. "For my idea, yes. We can work for the government and when we finish our university, we can have the government offer us the place for us to work. And just pay us a little money to feed ourselves and things like that. And so in this way we can pay back to them."

It seemed fair. And everyone in the room was willing to participate.

•   •   •

Literature

Zines still trickled in, and the young women continued to use them to describe how they felt to each other, what their provinces were like, who they wanted to become in the future. It was wonderful—heart-warming and sweet—but self-publishing was their tool by then. Still, the idea of zines spread quickly around the city, and I was invited to a meeting at a local literature organization on the future of publishing in Cambodia.

It was a small meeting—we all fit in a room together—and half foreigners. Very little support for publishing existed in Cambodia, and the various structures that publishing builds on or upholds were struggling, too. Few standards for education were set, whether on the learning or teaching side; no curriculum was established from which teachers and students could begin. Plus, of course, there was the fact that a several-tiered language formed the base of the national literature, with separate vocabularies for each strata of life form, from beast to royalty, as well as two separate ways of writing each, a modern and a traditional. All this was set within a culture trained to avoid the book, should one appear anyway, even before the Khmer Rouge made intelligence dangerous. A local old saw ran, "If you study philosophy, you will become a crazy person."

So an international organization devoted to literary freedom came to investigate whether or not an infrastructure for publishing could be created, and what it might take. A plethora of speakers were invited, and after my immersion in local self-publishing, I was fascinated. Each addressed a new and intriguing barrier to publishing in Cambodia.

Copyrights, for example. Legally, different sets of rules applied to layout, design, trademark, and intellectual property, of any given work. Some of these, in turn, were governed by the Ministry of Commerce; design and layout came under the jurisdiction of the Ministry of Trade; and general copyright was in the domain of the Ministry of Culture. Originally drafted in 1998, copyright laws were ratified for use only in 2003, when Cambodia joined the World Trade Organization. The Ministry of Culture opened a Department of Copyright in the middle of 2007, but confusion about the use and application of copyright still predominated, and the department had taken to sending out emissaries to describe the law.

"We have had very much attentions on this copyright thing, and it worry us a lot," the representative explained at the meeting.

Most discussion was devoted to music, because piracy was common. Cafes where you could burn your choice of CDs of Western music for five bucks, for example, were a decent source for new tunes, but more established pirated music shops—repackaged, with photocopied covers and all—were the norm. One speaker claimed such piracy would destroy the creativity of Cambodians, and the Ministry of Culture was trying to push for new legislation to protect creators. (I wasn't sure it was all so cut-and-dried as all that. One did not fail to write new songs when one could not download a Prince album for cheap, I knew. One failed to write new songs when one had no access to musical instruments, education, or time. Yet I was also seeing foreigners come in and use the confusion for their own benefit, which seemed a much more useful reason to enact new laws.)

An editor from the U.S. asked what recourse existed if a writer discovered her or his own work had been pirated. *Can you sue?* She asked. *Who do you call?* Violators could be fined for some million Riels, and then jailed for six to twelve months, an official explained. It didn't happen often, however. So far only filmmakers had stepped forward to complain of pirated DVDs.

Another major obstacle to publishing in Cambodia is that printing houses were rare, and most suppliers extranational: paper, ink, electricity, glue and other necessities were not locally available in large quantities, and shipping costs were high. Book publishing was just not cost effective. Which, in a population as destitute as Cambodia, is a major problem: If there was no personal gain to be had from creating books, how much of the country would get behind it?

An academic suggested the country embrace the e-book. Several murmured support, from both local and international camps. No one objected that the country didn't have widespread Internet access, nor computers outside of urban areas. This was a problem wholly separate from low national literacy rates.

I left baffled. Not only by the range of confusing issues I'd learned about, but also about the support for a digital solution. At the time, the dorm only had Internet access for a few hours each day, during which time the electricity may or may not have been working.

I pondered this as I headed back to Euglossa, happy my sisters already had a workaround for the difficulties of publishing in Cambodia. As I walked in, the dorm manager caught me and said *hi*. "Ms. Channy," I asked her. "What do you think about publishing books in Cambodia?"

"Many books," she said, "not good. They are foreign, or do not make sense, or have a bad aspect to them." Ms. Channy was big on morality, so books in which girls went on dates with boys were probably suspect.

"But this book," she continued, "That you write with all the girl?" She meant *New Girl Law*—or at least the book that would become *New Girl Law*. She'd been popping into our sessions regularly, and I'd asked her advice on some of the wording the young dorm residents had come up with. "I like it very much. It will be good."

I was surprised Ms. Channy had brought it up; I was also surprised that she had embraced the idea when Ryna had first suggested it. She'd told me once that she'd always wanted to do something similar, and that surprised me too. Ms. Channy was strongly in favor of keeping most Khmer traditions alive. She was a strong woman, only a year older than I was, and I respected her deeply. She was better prepared than I to know what future generations might find helpful.

And because of that, dear reader, I will tell you: That Ms. Channy had called *New Girl Law* important made me very happy.

•　　　•　　　•

Funding Should be Established in Support of Cultural Production
"We also want to establish funding for cultural production, which is writing, arts, music, dance…" Dina Sun articulated carefully. Her zine had been a wordless but colorful rendition of her childhood home. I had blown my entire copy budget on creating full-color versions to give away for free throughout the city and had to fundraise online to cover the costs of the round of publications we made next. It had been worth it.

"Exhibition?" Sotheary offered. We'd recently gone to an art show. They'd never been to one before.

"Concerts." This was Botum's request. We had all gone to a rock concert the night before and she'd been able to sneak her boyfriend into the crowd of giggling girls. She was in favor of concerts.

I flashed on a conversation I'd had with Leung the other day. She was coming out of the shower, finishing a tune. "Do you want to be a singer? You're very good at it." I said. She was. I'd accumulated several hours hanging around the bathrooms just listening to her shower or do her laundry. She had a stunning natural talent I'd never come across before, even with years under my belt as a music journalist.

"I don't know," she said brightly. "But I always think it can help me to decrease my tired. Or when I have a bath, a shower. Sometime when I water dish, I sing along, too." She meant wash. When she washes the dishes. I liked her term for it better.

"But you also dance," I noted. She was the first to leap into the apsara, at any reasonable occasion.

"I dance and I sing to make my life happy," she said.

It was what the future young women leaders of Cambodia wanted for each other.

5

LILI: I THINK THAT THIS WORLD IT MAKES ME DIE ALREADY

I have explained to you before that I did not have favorites among these young women, or rather that I had so many favorites that changed so frequently that even I could not be bothered to list them. This was mostly a lie: Lili was my favorite.

By American standards, Cambodian women tend to be beautiful, on average. Full of grace and charm and symmetry, with the tan skin prized by Hollywood actresses, but no darker. As Cambodia's advertising coffers filled with images of attractive people enjoying international products, demands to adhere to certain global beauty standards only increased. This was causing problems for young women, although not for the German and Vietnamese companies that stood to profit: Sales of skin whiteners were on the increase, and overuse had lead to health problems, even the death of one young woman preparing for her wedding.

It could not harm Lili. She was darker, and asymmetrical. She chided that she came from peasant stock, but this was true of everyone—for her, just more evident to the naked eye. "I black," she would say, pinching her skin. Her embrace of her difference was what mattered, and her enthusiasm for it.

"Hello, I nervous!" She exclaimed into my microphone gaily when I sat down to interview her. She clasped it like a karaoke singer.

I giggled, but also tried to signal seriousness. "Do not be nervous!" Being around her excited me, too. "I just want to ask you some questions about how your life has changed in the last couple of years, and how your family has changed by having you coming here."

"OK!" This, like everything else, excited Lili. "First, I came from Banteay Meanchey province. My father, he's a teacher, and my mother is a housewife, so this is our normal. Our family have one sister and one brother, is not big. No more than other people in the village, but a little bit hard because my family has illness? My sister is sick and cannot better. My family lost a lot of our money to buy her medicine. My family is not balance, because we need the money for my sister, and something that we house supply, like water and electricity, especially with the economic down, because everything is expensive. My family's just earn a normal wage."

Banteay Meanchey was a province in the Northwest of Cambodia, on the border with Thailand. It wasn't the poorest of the provinces—a few former Khmer Rouge still lived there in style—but it wasn't fancyland, either. If Lili lived there on a *normal wage* her parents probably took in only a buck or two, every day.

Lili had only been speaking English for a few months by then, and although I was uncomfortable with foreigners' oft-repeated descriptions of Phnom Penh as the Wild West, it did sort of apply to Lili's lawless approach to the language. I adored her mannerisms, and found myself adopting her turns of phrase whenever I could slip them in. She, for example, was the one who first called it a *chicken* instead of a *kitchen*. Now there's a generation of young English speaking Khmer women who believe the chicken to be the room in the house where you make rice, because an American goofball had used it earnestly on several occasions. Whoops.

"Has it been hard on your family having you live here?" I asked her. "Or easier, since they do not have to buy food for you or pay to have you in school?"

"It's changed a lot for me. Before, I want to study Japan language, but I change because I can't manage my time. Study Japan spend more time on remember and writing. It's hard for me to study a second or third language. I study at the Royal University of Law and Economic and my major is being in the Finance. It's a little too much arithmetic, but I try my best. I'm more interested in the financial market like the stock or bond? And another one, is I study at the University of Cambodia and the major is English Literature. I'm really grateful to study there because I'm a scholarship student."

Yes, she was pursuing finance and English literature degrees, but feeling bad because she couldn't also pick up Japanese. In a dormitory of overachievers she had no reason to believe this was unusual. "My living and my health is OK," she added, interrupting herself to laugh at that. "I happy and at peace, feel lucky that I'm here."

Although Lili and I had spoken frequently about her sister's illness, I did not understand what was wrong with her. "Because she is heart," Lili responded when I asked for clarification. "Related to the heart, I don't know what it's called in term of English. She stopped study."

"She lives at home with your parents? Is it hard having a sick person in the family?"

"Really hard. We lost the money to buy the medicine and we spend more with her living stuff. And her mind change a lot. Her place in the family is less, because we worry about her a lot even though she goes somewhere or she do something. That's why my family it seem to be happy, but not really when we think about her."

Health care in the provinces was bare bones when available, so medical conditions of almost any kind still, usually, signaled a short life. It was stressful. But Lili had been given some advantages and I wanted to hear more about them. "I remember you telling me once that when you were in high school your teacher never asked you for bribes."

"Yeah! I'm not good at speak but sometime I can do well with my communication and my style of learning," she said. "My relationship between me and teacher and all of the friend is good, and my teachers always know me and always ask me to do something or get something and I help them to manage the class. My mother, my family, cannot support me all the time because I study many major in high school like, four or five major. My teachers ask me to learn with them without paying any money. I say, *Thank you, but… I am not clever or smart but I try my best.* They say, *That it is OK, when you study here and you ask a good question, we all know that you are not a bad student.*"

It was a distinct honor, not to be bribed. Of foreigners too, it was the norm to be asked for money. One time a driver, who'd been salaried by an organization to drive me around for a week, charged me fifty dollars anyway. I was confused at first, and not clear what he was getting at. I doubted my agreement with the NGO—hadn't they told me they'd covered his salary? They had. Why would he need money? When I realized he just wanted more money, I gave him ten dollars and a strict talking to—I both did and did not want to be the American woman who can't be bothered to bend to local custom and fork over the requested fees. Lili, and all the girls, really, had been raised to pay these fees every day they wanted to stay in school, and as a regular consequence of being in the city. In that scenario it would have been unusual, maybe unthinkable, to refuse to pay the bribe teachers collected just so they could survive when government money failed to come on time, or at all. The very poor students who simply didn't have the money were pushed to the back of the classroom. But most paid.

"I have two or three teacher that instruct class without money. My favorite, and I respect her so much, is a role model for me." Lili explained, sighing. I had met this teacher once, very briefly, and she did truly seem to adore Lili. "She is a good leader, a good teacher, and a good sister too. She teach me how to open mind to new worlds. It come personally that she teach me without money. Maybe without her I can't find the way to Euglossa or to reach up my goal. My family also proud of her and admire her and respect her so much. My mom, she called her *Gold heart woman.* We all love her and respect her."

I had never heard the story of Lili's introduction to the dorm, but every young woman here had one, and told it with all the earnest exaggeration of a superhero origin tale. "What do you think you would be doing if your teacher did not tell you about Euglossa?" I asked.

"Hmm… maybe I can study at a university at Phnom Penh. Before, I wish every night, every week, every time that I think about university, I wish all the time. And before I know Euglossa, I cry one full night because my mother tell me, *You can't study at the university in Phnom Penh, I can't support you.* That night I cry full day, full night. It is a bad experience for me."

In situations like Lili's, parents frequently sent daughters off to work in the city. They had no choice, and other places for young women to work were rare. "Would you work in the garment factory?" I asked. That would at least be an income, however small. She could maybe earn a hundred dollars a month, if she worked overtime every day and skimped on food. She'd share an apartment with some other girls to save money and maybe be able to send half that home every month. However she'd be denying herself basic necessities to do it. "Or would you try to be a teacher?" I asked. This was even less reliable money, but much more worthy of Lili's intelligence and enthusiasm.

"I don't know what to do!" She howled in pain at the thought. "I think that this world it makes me die already. One week later, after the day

I cry, I walk it off and I'm alive again because my teacher have information about dorm. But it's not exactly like I pass. Because when I interview, I used to cry. The dorm manager ask me about my family. It affect my heart and I can't control myself and I cry again! It's the case that while I interview and I cry and I less confident and I hopeless. My teacher hope that I pass, but exactly we all know that I never pass because I cry in my interviews." She laughed at this for a long time.

"Except you did pass!" I exclaimed. I was as excited by her story as she was, even though I knew how it ended. Here, with me. In the dorm.

"Not then. I did not hear yet. I prepare to come to Phnom Penh then, but my mom changed her mind. Why I say like that: Because my mom asked me again, *Do you really want to study in Phnom Penh?* I don't say nothing. I just smile and walk past her and a few days later, she get me to Phnom Penh."

But her mom had poked some holes in Lili's confidence, and although the two found an uncle Lili could live with in Phnom Penh if she never heard back from Euglossa, she didn't know how expensive it would be to take care of herself in the big city. Food costs and tuition stacked up as the young woman from the province spent the day adjusting to what would become her new life, but she soon became scared that no one could help her if anything went wrong. By the end of that first day, Lili turned to her mom and said, *You're right. I don't want to do this.*

So the two got back on the bus to go home to Banteay Meanchey. "It's far from home and take forever, but two hour after we get on the bus we have a phone ring! I don't have a phone, just my mom that has, and she pick up the phone and I sit on the bus without soul. I saw that my body on the bus but my mind? That's not here! My mom always look at me and I know she worry about me." Lili was depressed, something she'd never experienced before. Or rather, she'd never experienced depression as something brought about by choices, opportunities, and loss. Only as a persistent daily side effect of poverty. Failure felt distinct and bad.

"Then the calling," she continued. "And my mom pick up, *Hello? Who who who and who and why and what?* And *This a call from Euglossa Foundation.* My mom say that, *Lili, Euglossa what?*, because she can't speak English and the call is in English."

When her mom handed Lili the phone the girl discovered that they were calling to invite her to live in the dorm. She screamed with joy, which I had heard almost daily for weeks. It was loud and arresting.

"On the bus were over fourteen people on there, and just me and my mom hold each other and stand. We're happy and I stand and we show our happiness on the bus. Everyone wonder, *Why two of them like that?*" Lili laughs again, long and hard, remembering the confusion of fourteen people on a bus in a province in Cambodia in the presence of joy. "I think, *My life is new again, I have a life of study. It's amazing for me to experience.*"

"You're crying a little bit now," I said gently.

"Yeah!" She said. Readers at home are probably getting a picture of Lili, kerchief in hand constantly, a never-ending stream of tears running down her face. But no, she actually didn't cry any more than the other girls. She laughed more, definitely, and louder. Her brightness shone straight out of her heart as if nothing else mattered. Which is probably why she kept mentioning the tears. She wanted to stop shedding them, to eliminate the bad, to banish it forever.

Her story continued, for she and her mom got off the bus, then and there, and turned around and went right back to Phnom Penh. Her third cross-country trip in two days. The first time she'd ever left home. "I don't want to talk about it. I want to ignore some question from anybody that ask me about my previous life, in high school. When they ask me about that, I'm very soft, I'm very surprised and I don't know what to tell them. I tell them it affect my heart. I will cry."

Gratefulness was important to Cambodians, as evidenced by *Katanho*, an epic film on the subject of expressing gratefulness through dedicated fits of weeping. That's what I got out of it. We had all watched it together, all thirty-two of us on a single vinyl couch in the heat of late evening. It was a difficult thing, to withstand so much gratefulness.

"What do you think you have learned living in Euglossa?" I asked.

"I've learned a lot. Especially food." She laughed, and gave me a wicked grin.

I, too, was devoted to food pedagogy, and she was always quick to capitalize on it, offering me bites of new kinds of rice, or fresh takes on green mango. Potato for dessert. Once, a fried grasshopper. *It from Banteay Meanchey!*, she had demanded, and how was I to refuse that?

"The way that I cook, the way that I speak, it changed me a lot. Before the first year, I had a stomachache because I can't adapt to another food that they cook. It make me go to hospital one time last year."

"Were you not eating enough? Or did you have trouble digesting?" The young women in the dorm then still operated under a poverty mentality. They refused to explain to dorm staff that the money they were given to live on couldn't, sometimes, cover both toilet paper and food expenses. They usually went without the former, but when the economy started floundering, the cost of a tank of propane nearly doubled, and the costs of drinking water, too. For a while, the students had to choose between purchasing drinking water, buying the propane that would allow them to boil out impurities in tap water and cook food, get toilet paper, or afford the food itself. Emerging from poverty was no easy feat, and Lili felt the creaks and groans of a developing nation almost daily.

"Because I cannot adapt. Sometimes I can't eat it! I try all the thing. Everything is good if you think about the good thing and the benefit of them," she said. She meant, *Even illness is OK if you let it change you.*

I asked what she wanted to do in the future.

"I want to study abroad!" She said, excitedly. Of course she said it excitedly. "I wish and I dream more about my life. My mom always ask me the thing about marriage, because I'm the older sister in the family." They would traditionally have needed to make sure she was married before finding a husband for her younger sister, which I imagined her family might be eager to do. "I told them don't think about it. *I'm OK*, I say to them. *I will be good for you, I will bring something that you like for you. I will be get everything that I can do for our family to be better.* So they respect my idea. They say, *OK, do what you want.*" It wasn't clear from her tone if they were disappointed or concerned, only that she had sought their permission not to marry, for now, and they had granted it.

"I'm not exactly know that I can continue Ph.D. when I come back to Cambodia or work for a NGO or another organization. Then, one year or two years, maybe I think again about marriage, to respect my family law." She laughs, and corrects herself. "Not exactly like that, but maybe I will choose someone to support me, to guideline me, to do everything I dream about and reach the goal to get there, not just about love but about work about life, about our study lives."

Ugh. I'd been looking for that as a strong woman in the U.S. for over thirty years and hadn't found it yet. "Do you think that will be difficult, to find a partner like that in Cambodia?"

"Really hard! We just choose, choose, choose, when we pick up one? It's not really how we do. So we have to set the criteria for ourselves, not highs, not lows, but exactly love of family, support us, and do something that can be our life, our family, and our community."

She had a fairly strong understanding of love as part of a system of economic and emotional support that was rare in the generation of Cambodians raised by Khmer Rouge regime survivors. As I had with the other girls, I asked what her parents were doing during Pol Pot time.

"Oh, my father, he teach part time to find more money," She said. The Khmer Rouge had largely trained and organized in and near her province in the 1970s, so her family wasn't subject to some of the upheavals other girls' families were. Her family were *old people*, in the parlance of that day, and therefore continued on with their lives with minimal disruption. It was *new people*, from the cities, whose lives changed most suddenly.

"Do you think that the fact that he lived through that time changed him?" I asked.

"Maybe some. Some family that have children and they're rich they, like, rent my father to teach their children in the evening one hour or two hour? My father had to do. Yeah." She scowled. He hadn't enjoyed the work. "But now he is school director in primaries school. He not earn a lot of money like teaching before so he try other ways to make money. Also my mother? She open the small business selling a book, pen, souvenir. She earn a little bit more money, and pull it together, mix it together, and can help me and support me too."

"How did she meet your father?"

"She study, and live in Battambang and my father was going to move to Banteay Meanchey to teach there," she explained. Lili's grandmother, who also owned a small business, had offered the man a place to live at her son's house, Lili's mom's uncle. Apparently he'd also caught sight of Lili's mom, and one day her grandmother announced that Lili's mom would no longer attend school. "I don't whether they fall in love or something else, but both of my uncle's family and my mom's family saw that my father is good. He can make a good family for my mom and they get married," she explained.

"And then you were born…" I prodded, sure this would excited her.

"Yeah!" She said. It did. "So now I'm here for you."

We both laughed for a long time, at the joy of being there, together.

6

New Girl Laws

Domestic Violence Should be Prosecuted and Reported by Authorities and Neighbors, and Perpetrators Should be Punished.

"One of the things that worries me about the *Chbap Srei* is the parts that say that if your husband wants to hurt you, you should let him," I said flatly one night.

I had been waiting for the dorm residents to bring it up but they hadn't. Their reticence was partially due to their disinterest in acknowledging just how awful Cambodian culture can be, to me, an outsider. After all, the standard line on Americans was that if they found you unpleasant they might not offer assistance. Not that my young women were that calculated in their dealings with me—I knew, in fact, that they wanted both far less and far more from me than money—but a dependency was built into the fabric of our two cultures, and you could see it mirrored in every transnational program created: the trade agreements, the military deals, the aid programs. Yet I believe the girls were also hanging on to some shred of hope that I didn't know what the *Chbap Srei* said. I wanted to dispel that belief. How could we trust each other if we did not communicate honestly?

Chenda had started nodding even before I finished my sentence. "Yes." She said. Then: "No, no, no."

I didn't want to assume what she meant.

"I think if the man hits the woman, the man should think that, *How could it be if he was the woman and someone hit him?* Something like that," Ryna said.

"Keep peace," Dina Sun added. She hadn't yet taken a seat, so her tallness was exaggerated in the room of relaxing women.

"Keep peace. Yes." I wanted to tread carefully. Their Buddhist tendencies were clashing with their desire to write useful policy. "My worry is that these are all probably rules that already exist in Cambodia, right? Social, or legal rules. You should keep peace, you should consider the feelings of others? And still, men hit women, a lot. So I wonder if there is a way we can say it even more clearly?"

"Like: If the man hit the woman, the police will bring him in to jail?" Dina Sun asked.

To my surprise, everyone laughed. Comedy gold.

"We already have a law against domestic violence," Chenda said. It had been passed only three years beforehand, in 2005. "We punish already…"

"Punish by going to jail?" Sotheary asked in her sweet voice. She genuinely didn't know.

I had read the reports and had a slightly clearer sense of whether or not the perpetrators of domestic violence went to jail. "In all cases?" I challenged Chenda.

"Sometimes not," she admitted. A large-sample study from the *Journal of Family Violence* published the next year found that twenty-two percent of Khmer women reported experiencing domestic violence after the age of 15. The garment industry's growth in the country, heavily reliant on a female workforce, was thought to be a contributing factor, leading to male frustration and jealousy. It was also, arguably, the reason domestic violence allegations were coming to light at all: Women working outside the home meant they had contact with people besides their abusers, and a degree of economic clout that bolstered a sense of self-preservation. Still, four years later in 2012, only three hundred and twenty rapes would be reported in the Kingdom. In response to one incident in the Kandal province, when a disabled 19-year-old was attacked in a banana field one evening, the police chief blamed the victim, suggesting to the *Cambodia Daily* that the young woman shouldn't have been out so late.

"So domestic violence should be prosecuted," Dina Sun stated, "by whoever sees it occur."

"Yeah," Chenda agreed. I wrote it on the board.

•   •   •

Land Under Development

It was true that the nation was in the midst of an economic boom, the likes of which the country had never before experienced, but the flipside of this was that people kept getting in the way of progress with unprofitable demands for rights. You could almost hear the silent inclusion of the word *pesky* in government proclamations regarding people who refused to leave their land when evicted.

Like everything else in the country, land was a confusing issue in the Kingdom. It was only fairly recently that squatters' rights were defined, whereby anyone who had been in possession of a piece of land for five years could claim ownership of it, but it was tricky because in some cases deeds were misfiled or unissued or never signed or simply lost. Governmental corruption had not quelled with development, and as the population of Cambodia grew, and greater international business interests demanded more and more work space on Cambodian soil, it remained easy to convince someone to lose a piece of paper, or demand with firepower that it had never existed.

In early 2008 one group had managed to coalesce around community goals and stave off several separate illegal eviction notices, Group 78. We drove by it one day on the way to a meeting and there appeared to be a hubbub. Later we found out that a grenade had exploded in the area, and organizers were concerned that the group's dedication to the fight might be wavering.

Group 78, in response to another eviction notice, had just created a neighborhood redevelopment plan that adhered to both the law and the government's demands on the neighborhood. They had constructed it with an urban planning team hired through local universities, and had presented it reasonably and carefully to the officials who would really rather their earlier shows of force had worked. It looked at the time as if the plan could go through, but the explosion had scared folks off.

Organizers knew that if Group 78 walked away, the battle for land in Cambodia might be lost. As the sole group to emerge victorious from these skirmishes, Group 78 was an important symbol. If they walked away, organizers feared they would never be able to convince another Cambodian to stand up for their rights. What Group 78 did, really, was remind folks that at least some people retained a basic critical awareness of the law. That was what was at stake. The meeting with organizers was short—so would be Group 78. The following year all one hundred and forty six families would be cleared from land claimed by a local developer after land titles were never produced by government officials. Most families were given $8,000 USD for their homes. I was only there to learn as much as I could so I could explain to the young women in the dorm what was going on while they were in school.

When I returned that afternoon, Ms. Channy caught me walking in the door. I told her where I had been, discussing housing and land rights with Group 78 supporters and organizers.

In response, Ms. Channy told me she and the dorm's founders were preparing to expand—that is, they were looking for land for a second dormitory. They had been traveling the city looking for sites, but had so far found the cost of land prohibitive when not astronomical. One site she described as, "Very expensive. And under water." The other plot had a price tag of hundreds of thousands of dollars.

The third site under consideration was just next door, where the man lived who sold gasoline in plastic tanks out of his front yard. When he had first mentioned to Ms. Channy that he planned to sell it six months previous, the price tag had been $80,000 USD. The asking price had since jumped to $120,000 USD.

It was a lot, the dorm manager agreed, but it sort of didn't matter to her. She said she knew nothing about appropriate land costs, since she and her husband and two young daughters still lived with her parents, and would probably continue to for the rest of their lives.

•   •   •

Corruption Laws Should be Established, Enforced, and Respected.
Our next chicken session started pretty openly. "Can you guys think of anything else? Anything that would make your lives easier right now, that we should put in to the new rules?"

A moment of silence, then: "Stop corruption."

There was something about being in a small room with so many young women learning to be outspoken that made me both excited and anxious. I flashed on nature footage from some documentary I'd watched as a girl—from a distance away a calm brown, a soothing hum. Up close, uncountable bees each clamoring for a different demand. Even from outside the doorway, I bet everything appeared peaceful. The undercurrent of the room, however, was pure energy.

I didn't know how to harness it to stop corruption. "How would we put that into the list?"

"Make corruption law."

The lawyers chimed in: "No, the corruption law already drafted, but it's not established. It's been drafted about sixteen years."

A year later this law would be established, and even occasionally enforced. Rarely however, I would come to believe, respected. Dina Sun predicted this: "It should not just be establish," she argued artfully. "It must also be enforce. Respect."

·   ·   ·

Haircut Like a Boy

Lili and Amoun and I went to get haircuts at the shop down the street. It didn't go very well. At first the ladies refused to cut my hair.

"Umm, they are worried about your mind," Amoun said. "They only cut girls' hair."

"Amoun, I don't know what that means, but it does not sound good. I assume you know I am a girl?"

She laughed, and said, "They do not want."

"Oh." They did not want to cut my hair. Because they are worried that I am crazy for wanting it to be short. Because only boys have short hair. "You can tell them that I only want the back trimmed, and even if it looks really bad I will not care. Tell them that I am American, and therefore have no sense of style." I said.

She translated. "Oh, OK," she said. "They will try."

We waited, because we all wanted to get our hair cut at the exact same time, so the entire shop needed to clear out for us. This was important to us because this is what sisters do. Things, together. I'd never had sisters and it made me feel uncomfortable and special. Amoun and Lili were completely at ease, all the time. Their confidence was staggering.

Next door, someone was running the soda shop, a large orange cooler open in a doorway. Lili leaned against me and looked at the proprietor. "I feel pity for him," she said. "He want to be a girl. He always wear the skirt, and walk like a girl, only spend time with girl."

"Is he gay?" I asked. She sat up with a straight spine and blinked. Then looked at me oddly. Later I realized that my comfort with his ambiguous gender presentation was, itself, a problem. To overlook the fact that he was, just then, wearing a skirt to ask about his sexuality struck her as mildly offensive. How could I not respect the strict division between male and female? Perhaps something really was wrong with my mind.

"I do not know," she said. "He want to be a girl."

"Is it common here?" I asked. Pulling my thing of: in the U.S., we do it like this. "At home, it is kind of common. For boys to want to be girls and for girls to want to be boys." The language is tricky, of course: Sometimes boys do not *want* to be girls. They just have to transition, because it is the physical process through which one's mind can align with one's body parts. Still, explaining to Lili in that moment that some people are born in the wrong body—sitting there, in a hair cuttery for women where I have just demanded they cut my hair *like a boy's* even though *they are worried about my mind*—this would not have gone over so well. How would I respond to the follow-up question, sure to come, all sweetness and innocence after that: *Do you want to be a boy?* I was watching it form behind Lili's eyes. I had already been accused of it in a milder form. And once my haircut was complete they could have no doubts.

The truth is that I did not want to be a boy. Of course I did not want to be a boy. I would have had to leave the dorm and all my sisters and I loved being female. However it was undeniable that every single thing about my life would have been easier if I had been born into the body upon which my culture—not to mention Cambodia's —heaps all privilege.

In a small way, yes, that was what the haircut was about. I had a slightly androgynous gender presentation that skewed to masculine against the backdrop of Southeast Asia. If I didn't have the freedom of cutting my hair short and traveling around the world by myself as an American woman, I probably would have questioned my gender presentation. Very deeply.

"I do not know," Lili said. She shook her head at him. "*Srei sros,*" she said, the term for a trans woman that actually meant *charming girl.* A synonym was *sak veng*. Long hairs. "He does not have friend. I feel pity for him, because the government. Because later, will he marry? He will be lonely."

"Hmm," I said. "Maybe he will find other people to talk to, soon." I kept thinking: Oh, this person needs to leave Cambodia. Spend time with people who can understand. And then I would realize: I am sitting here watching this person's income accumulate. There's no chance in the world to leave Cambodia. What was I thinking? That's expensive. Later, I would meet more trans women. It was rare, but happened, that folks born into male bodies in Cambodia lived as women, transitioned. Became happy. The beverage seller would find them too, I hoped.

A few minutes later a woman with dyed hair wearing a purple shirt and taking a moment off from tying extensions into some other girl's hair agreed to take a razor to the back of my head. Lili and Amoun were already seated in chairs, having their hairs cut lovingly while I just sat stock still, waiting for the sole lady in the place with the *cojones* to trim my hair. In the end, it only took a few seconds.

Normally, elsewhere, a haircut went for one dollar. This was a pretty ritzy shop, so here it was three to five dollars. But *here*, Lili told me several times, *they are very good*. (She did not mention that they were also a little judgmental.) So when the woman in the purple shirt was done she said, *OK for you*. It looked great. Then she said something quickly in Khmer.

Amoun translated into English. "You do not have to pay," she said. I had understood that part, although I thought it was weird.

What she hadn't translated for me, which I had just enough Khmer to pick up myself, was what the woman in purple had said next: *Do not say where she cut her hair. We do not want people to know.*

·   ·   ·

Local Production Should be Supported by Reducing Taxes and Decreasing Imports

"I think we should support our local production," Amoun said.

"Local production, good. How—do you have an idea for how we should do that?" I asked. I was officially out of my element.

"Take less tax from local products and more from imported products? Also import less from the other countries." Amoun had clearly thought about this already, thank the Buddha.

My job was getting really easy. They had all clearly formulated ideas for how the development of Cambodia could better foster health and well-being for Cambodians, and for Cambodian young women. I had pretty much become their stenographer.

．　　　．　　　．

The Noise-Making Festival

Some kind of early-morning noise-making festival woke me up the next morning, monk-chanting down the block that was So. Not. Peaceful. I wanted to punch someone. OK, that is an exaggeration. Monk-chatter is actually quite nice, but mornings start here at five (sleeping late is seven) and the racket had been going down since 4:30 a.m.

I was thinking of the time we'd watched *Tum Teav*. Being the sole comfort to a sobbing couch full of thirty-two young Cambodian women is not an experience likely to leave you quickly. Specifically, I was thinking about romantic love. It wasn't something I did a lot. I dated for the adventure of it, both in Cambodia and at home. What did a killer do in his free time? A cop? A rapper? I thought of sex as another way to learn, another thing to giggle about. Love was different, rare. The opposite of adventure, really. Accepting instead of challenging, comforting instead of abrasive. It could mould a person, all the same.

The girls talked about love—true love—a lot. More than I did at their age; more, even, than the girls I couldn't stand growing up. *Boy crazy*, I called them. The term was insufficient to describe my young friends. Yet arranged marriages still happened. Not always between Cambodians, either. Sometimes as part of a grander business plan, sometimes to foreigners. Eventually a law would be passed that demanded foreigners only marry the oldest single woman in a household, so common had it become for the youngest to leave the house first. Where did romantic love come into play then? Parental pressure to get married, whether to a chosen partner or one chosen for them, was heavy on the Euglossa girls. But the idea of romantic love persisted. Among boys, too, although the way that romance was packaged for boys—the most beautiful girl you come across in your travels is clearly the one for you, and you must pursue her at any cost, as in *Tum Teav*—is different than the way it was packaged for girls—a man will come into your life, and there may well be only one, as you must remain close to home and hard-working until marriage. These are quite different. For boys, romance included choice. For girls, it hinged on patience.

Which brought me back to the noise-making festival. I had a lot of time to ponder it, since it turned out to be a two-day wedding ceremony. (*Riep Kahr: married*, they explained to me in their I'm-teaching-you-Khmer-now-voices.) Wedding ceremonies used to last seven days and now only last two, my roommates explained.

"Why did that change?" I asked.

"Because of society," Lili told me.

"But what did society do to make it change?" I asked.

"They think that when we have seven day, we do not work. When we have two, we have time to enjoy, but we can go back and work," she said.

Amoun told me it was an effort toward integration with other cultures. *The seven-day ceremony was too long, and now Cambodian society can accommodate other ways,* she said.

Chenda put it a different way. "Glow. Ball. Eye. Zay. Shun," she said. And it was true; there was a market aspect to all the romance. Valentine's Day geegaws had gone on sale in December.

●   ●   ●

Savior

Something uncomfortable was starting to happen at the edges of our shiny girl empire. The dorm and the atmosphere it created was still heavenly, no question. Outside its doors, the jobs and opportunities the dorm fostered for Cambodians was a smart use of foreign aid. The Euglossa founder was well loved for it, and respected. Deservedly.

Occasionally, however, feelings for him—a white American man— moved beyond genuine appreciation toward a less clear emotion. One day, portraits of him appeared on the walls in each of the three study areas in the dorm; I was told the girls had requested them. I'd never heard them express such a wish, although I wouldn't have been surprised. They adored him unflinchingly. They called him dad, in the same way that they called me sister. This was occasionally confusing, when we were discussing their fathers, for example. Yet it was an honorific, an endearment. It was not troubling on its own.

Once the pictures were up, something changed. It was difficult not to read them as altars. They were used as such, in a way. Not for praying, exactly, but as a secular reminder, a way to pay respects. Conversations about the dorm, about the future, about economic development in the country thereafter made visual reference to the pictures. Our all-girl haven acquired an onlooker. The tone of discussions about the dorm in the presence of these images moved quickly from adoration to adulation. A new vocabulary emerged, nearly frenetic in gratitude. It was strange.

I don't know how much of it was the pictures themselves, actually. Perhaps they only acted as a reminder of privilege for this first large group of young women who were going to college together. But these young women were Cambodian, tan-skinned, and poor, and being reminded several times per day that they wouldn't be where they were without a foreign savior.

The White Savior Industrial Complex had been developing its own logic in Cambodia since UNTAC, when wealth disparity was raced and nationalized, and economic development meant catering to internationals. Or maybe it had been there all along, something UNTAC had merely made evident, another downside of colonialism and empire. As I'd experienced being white, and in Cambodia, it didn't matter whether or not you intended to take advantage of the privileges afforded your foreignness, your Westernness. Advantage was almost foist upon you, and rejecting it took effort. It wasn't the founder's intention, in other words, this reverence. It was just how things tended to work for white folks, especially white men, in Cambodia. Ex-pats loved it.

I said nothing. These young women had enough to consider. Yet when the founder's daughter came to visit, she was perturbed. "Anne," she said, "Does anything about these picture strike you as weird?"

We discussed it at length. Afterwards, she took them down, packed them up, and placed them in Ms. Channy's office.

"Ms. Channy," she said. "The way the girls treat these pictures makes me uncomfortable." *As strong women ourselves,* she explained to the dorm manager, including all three of us in the first person plural, *we all understand the need to forge an environment of self-sufficiency.*

"I see," Ms. Channy said.

But the next day the pictures were back up.

. . .

A Minimum Wage Should be Established for Work Done in the Public Service
"Do you have a minimum wage in the Kingdom?" I asked.

"It's not enough," Lili said.

"It's not enough to fulfill their families," Narin clarified. Sort of.

Hm. Maybe they didn't know what minimum wage was. This could be helpful. More helpful than the time I explained what a brownie was. Or at least *as* helpful, since that had turned out to be pretty significant. "In this country, do you have something like a lowest amount of money you can be paid to do any job? It is sometimes based on the smallest amount of money it would take to live in your country." In fact, the minimum wage wasn't often calculated with a living wage in mind, but at least it gave us a way to talk about money.

"Sometimes. Soldiers. Garment workers."

"So you have it in certain industries, but not for everyone?" I asked.

"No. But there would still be poverty."

"Who would still be in poverty?"

"Construction workers." Someone said.

"Teacher, cleaner…"

"Guard, security guard." This last from Maly. She did not say much in our discussions but she listened intently.

They had named almost all the entry-level jobs that were not in the service industry. "Are there any jobs that are above poverty level, where you can earn enough money to live in Cambodia?" I asked.

"Work in the government and in the company that can afford their life," Narin answered.

"So, government or for-profit business. Well, it looks to me like we should talk about a basic standard amount of pay. For everyone."

"Like all jobs? Yes." Narin concurred. At the time, international trade agreements helped bolster the garment industry wages, and national laws would uphold the soldiers' pay at a certain level. It seemed not to have occurred to these young women that the act of being employed itself could be construed as a protectable right, compensated not exclusively through private agreements between individuals, but through a nationally established standard.

"Luckily we have already established corruption law, so all of the money that is going into Cambodia will be accounted for. People can use that, maybe, to start paying minimum wage." Ryna said. Then she put the pen behind her ear like someone who has just won a court case in a Hollywood movie.

"Yes! But I'm not an economist," I reminded her.

"I am," Maly said. She looked up from some numbers she was running in her notebook. "It OK."

•   •   •

Dessert

Amoun planned to surprise us all with a dessert one afternoon. I had to run out, so I asked if she needed any ingredients.

"No, No." She said. "I have everything I need. This"—and she pointed to a small pumpkin—"some coconut milk, some spice. Some eye of pork. Mmmmm. Delicious." She patted her tummy.

"What?"

"Coconut milk. Spice. Eye. You do it like this in United States?" Amoun was holding her arm out over the ingredients of the feast she was about to prepare, completely sure it was normal. *You do it like this in United States?* and *You do it like this in Cambodia?* had become the way we introduced cultural differences. How we talked about dating, for example, or makeup. How we talked about being women in the world. I had stayed away from doing much cooking, largely because I did not want to have a discussion where I explained that I did not, in the United States, normally eat the eye of a pig in a dessert.

"Ummm, Amoun," I said. Kind of appalled. "No. Why would we do that?"

"Oh, delicious." She drew it out, to entice me.

"Umm. Amoun." I said. I was unsure what to do. If there was going to be pig eyeball in my food, I did not want to know about it. I would eat it, but I didn't want to know about it first.

Then she started laughing, really really hard.

•   •   •

Laws as Written Shall be Enforced by Everyone, Including Lawmakers
There was no real narrative to how we came to this rule. It's just that, we eventually realized that it was missing, and its lack seemed to be the biggest impediment to the greatest volume of freedom the young women in the room felt they deserved. On our last gathering together in the chicken, I read the collected rules all the way through. They were beautiful, and we all felt proud.

Then brave and smart Ryna said this: "Laws as written should be enforced by everyone, even the law makers." The room's relief and happiness were our unanimous assent.

7

Sotheary: The Other Thing is Sexuality in Phnom Penh

"I am the student of accounting at University of Management in Cambodia," Sotheary began into my microphone. You could already see that her education at Euglossa was pushing her in new directions. A few short months beforehand she had been a shy quiet girl from the provinces who wore shirts with cartoon animals on them every chance she got. Now she held the microphone sternly, like a BBC reporter. Certainly, she giggled as much as she used to, but now she emanated a sense of professionalism while doing it.

Sotheary was my last scheduled interview. We sat on the precipice of a coming global recession, but Cambodia's economy, for the most part, was still on an upswing. The country would probably always be balanced precariously between want and comfort, and that made me wonder where these young women might end up. Sotheary was studying accounting, so she seemed the perfect person to query. "Are you concerned about jobs after you graduate?" I asked.

"Yes. Sure. We have thought about the jobs because, in my school we don't allow to work as we studying, so that when we graduate we don't have much experience. When I graduate from the bachelor degree, maybe a little bit difficult to find a job. But I think that's OK, because we have volunteer and internship with the organization and company. I think that—I hope that—one day I will get a job. It might be difficult. With accountant, it's not like in the United States. Where accountants are like the lowest and not that smart? But in Cambodia, because the government and also the investor come and the bank and also the people being invested … I think maybe they will have a job for me."

Sotheary was pointing out that there were simply less people in accounting in Cambodia than in a developed country. Any financial infrastructure that would have supported such a practice had been ransacked under the Khmer Rouge when money was abolished. The wealthy had always been notoriously disinterested in storing riches in a location outside the home anyway. Traditionally, wives wore the entirety of their families' wealth as gold jewelry, and informal moneylenders, like Maly's mom, filled any other needs that may arise. This hadn't changed once the Cambodian Riel was reissued in 1980, nor when banks started to emerge again. Even today, over ninety-five percent of the adults in the country do not have bank accounts.

But it wasn't just Sotheary: I feared the job search would be crushing for all the young women. "What are the other girls doing to make sure they will be in a good position to get a job?"

"Some join the school club. Leung join them all. She is a joiner." Sotheary laughed openly. She didn't mean it as an insult, and was actually laughing at a word she thought she might have invented. It was a word we used to sling at each other in my high-school days too, where the pressure to be a *leader* was just as pronounced as it was in the dorm.

Sotheary just loved to have fun. She was always the first to leap up to dance, and the first to fall down again, giggling. It made her chosen field all the more strange to consider. "Why did you want to study accounting?" I asked her.

"Exactly the first reason is that I am good at maths and all of my brother, my cousin, they saw that. Accounting is better to find a job."

"But here in the dorm you are also planning to be a leader of Cambodia. How will you accomplish that goal and still be an accountant? What will that look like?"

"The first time I ever read about accountant, I had a talk with Ms. Channy about it. She said, *If you want to become a leader, you can study accounting and then when you finish bachelor degree, you can go to master degree, and you can do whatever you want if you have the confidence to do it.* It is not like studying law, where you can become a leader in government or something like that."

I was beginning to grasp something that would later become more clear, that leadership, as it was being taught to these girls, had a distinctly masculine edge. The skills on offer were starting to embrace a certain strong and visible and loud aggression. Which didn't always jive, it seemed, with the Cambodian notion of social change. It was competitive, not transformative.

Sotheary was too Cambodian for it. She intended to lead by being very good at what she did. "If you didn't come to live at Euglossa, what do you think you would be doing right now?" I asked her.

"It is the question that I have thought about, because before when I graduate from high school, I got the grade C. I want to go to the scholarship and grade C is like …" her voice trailed off and she made a face of disgust. A C wasn't going to get her a scholarship. "My mom talked to me about it. She told me that she want me to continue my studies into college, but if I didn't get the scholarship to study, I would go back to the province and wait until she own the money. She need to earn money to support me to study at school and also my situation in Phnom Penh. I would need to rent house or something and it is very expensive."

"You would need money for tuition and for rent." One of the more expensive schools in Cambodia cost three hundred dollars per semester; one of the cheaper rooms I knew of cost twenty five dollars per month to rent, although that was garment factory housing, and I doubted she could find anything that cheap. With food costs rising well beyond two dollars per day in the city, this future accountant was looking at annual bills of about $2,000 USD. In a country where salaries averaged $720 USD per year. She could do the math.

"One of the other thing is sexuality in Phnom Penh?" Sotheary meant both an interior sense of sexuality—how we used the term in the U.S.—and an external one, more like sexualization. The latter most often took forms of gender-based harassment and sexual assault. Common in families too, the girl told me, was the fear that men will convince young women who live alone to have premarital sex with them, limiting the chance that they will marry afterwards, thus achieve any kind of economic security. Valentine's Day was coming up, a holiday devoted, the girls honestly believed, to consenting to sex with young men. It had been the topic of several discussions that had started like this: *In United States, you must to have sex with a boy who gives you a flower, or is optional?* They were asking for friends, mostly, but soon would face decisions about their own sexuality. This application of the term—American feminist sexuality, or the notion that young women can healthily and happily explore their own pleasure—was not commonly used. More frequently uttered was the Khmer aphorism, *Men are diamonds and women are cloth.* Men, in other words, could go through the worst shit imaginable, and be restored to luster with only a rinsing. Women, however, would be permanently ruined. It was a phrase Sotheary heard more than once in rebuttal to her desire to find an apartment in the city while she was in school. It wasn't her only barrier. "The other is I need to find a job and find money to support my study."

"So if you didn't come to the dorm, then you still would have gone to college..."

"Not really," she said earnestly.

"Because you would not have been able to support yourself? And your family might not allow it?"

"Yes, too many things. Especially, it's money."

"So," I didn't want to push her too hard on this what-if scenario—it was clearly a point of agitation for all the girls I'd interviewed—but hundreds of thousands of girls in the country didn't have the opportunities she did, and Sotheary was sill close enough to them to know what their plans were. She had been an active participant in the process of imagining a new future for Cambodia with *New Girl Law*, but for those discussions to be effective, we had to be clear on the present of Cambodia, outside of the dorm. "If you had stayed in your own province, would you get a job there?"

"It doesn't have a job there. If I stayed with my family I need to do the family there. My family and maybe go to factory."

"Is there a factory nearby?" Most young women were sent from the provinces to Phnom Penh to work in the factories because few, if any, were located outside of the city surrounds.

"Before no, but now it has. My family want me to study and maybe they push me but maybe working too hard to support me to study."

There were seven people in her family, including her grandmother and parents. "Are you the youngest?" I asked.

"No, I am the second from oldest. Middle. All brothers." She laughed.

"You were the only girl? Was it lonely?"

"Sure." She drew it out and laughed again. Being raised as the only girl had given her sense of humor a sharp edge that I loved, but she clearly questioned whether or not she fit into an all-boy crowd. When she had arrived at the dorm to discover a space where only women lived, she told me, "I am very happy! Because I want sister and also want younger sister and older sister, so when I come here? I have it!" Not that she wasn't still close with her family. "My brother, he does the stuff of microfinance at a small organization in Phnom Penh now. He graduate in 2004."

"Besides him," I asked, "Is everyone else still living at home?" Her family lived in the Kandal province, a province that entirely surrounds, but doesn't include, the capital.

"Yeah," she said. She was learning a lot at the dorm, which also meant she was growing away from them a bit. "The first time that I came here, I have changed my characteristic and also my attitude because I live with a girl and I want to live with the community with all the girls here. I have learned about the life before they come to the dorm. It is very different from each other. We have some fight through the difficult situation." I thought again of the documentary I'd watched on beehives: only monochrome and soothing from a distance.

Life in the provinces seemed homogenous enough to me, but each was of course vastly different from the others. Obviously they would be, I just didn't know how to perceive the differences. I couldn't even tell one kind of rice from another, and there were seven thousand distinct varieties. "After meeting all the girls here, do you feel like your family's situation was difficult or easy or normal?"

"Very difficult." She didn't need to clarify that that meant they were poor. "I spend, like, it might not be much money for the others, but it is very much for me and my family. I spend my money and my mother sometimes she blame me, *Why you out spend so much money?* And this is spent for food."

Once I had taken Sotheary out to meet some friends of mine, fans of her zine, actually. Some Western, some Southeast Asian, all participants in the global art market. We met for dinner. I was paying for her meal, but Sotheary didn't want to order any food. I couldn't figure out why. She'd been talking about hamburgers for weeks, imagining what they might be, comparing them to her favorite foods, fantasizing about having both bread and beef in your mouth at the same time. They had a hamburger at the restaurant we were at, for five bucks. "It *expensive!*" she whispered at me loudly when I leaned in. "For one food!"

On the whole, though, she said the dorm was "very helpful for me because I learn how to communicate. So I become more confident and talk with the people all around me and also like with you, foreigner. Before I didn't want to talk but I came—" she breaks off, laughing, looking at me pointedly "—now I can talk to you."

"But you've always talked to me," I said. It was true. Sotheary had never once been shy in my presence.

"Sure! But before, you know, when I was in high school, one foreigner came to my school and I didn't want to talk to him and I just stand and look at his face. I didn't want to say, *Hello.*"

"Well now you are very friendly. Also however, there are many more tourists than there used to be." Tourism in Cambodia had increased exponentially every year.

"Exactly. The people that come to Cambodia might be touring, for one example. Also the people that come to help by teaching, however they want to get money but they help Cambodia by teaching or just come to visit or something like that ..." She was referring not only to tourism, then, but to volunteerism, or voluntourism, really—young adults who wanted to devote time to working in foreign nations but sought some kind of wage to make their commitment sustainable. It was sensical, from a certain perspective. When you offer labor and skill to furthering a situation of social justice you should be no less compensated than when you donate labor and skill to increasing profit margins for widgets, for example. At the same time, most of the young people coming to Phnom Penh had an outsized notion of both their skill level and the value of their labor to an economy where people earned less than a thousand dollars per year. I'd seen plenty of folks expecting close to a minimum U.S. wage—around twenty times the national average—to teach folks skills that would never earn locals anything close to that salary. It was preposterous. To me, at least.

Sotheary was in favor of it. "It is good for them to help Cambodia or, like you, to come to teach us and help the women in Cambodia. That's good! But the other foreigners they come and make the problem in Cambodia, like say something about the king or something, that would be headline." Traditional hostilities, such as those between Thailand and Cambodia, often bubbled up. A Thai actress in 2003 had allegedly claimed the Temples of Angkor Wat to be Thai creations, reputedly saying she wouldn't set foot in the country until the land was redesignated Thai soil. The statement was never verified, but Prime Minister Hun Sen shot back that she was "not worth a few blades of grass near the temple" and riots broke out in Phnom Penh. Thai businesses and the embassy were burned to the ground. Foreign leaders of NGOs occasionally came and spoke out against government leaders, too.

The prime minister was beginning to make public statements in prohibition of criticism, making a lesson out of one or two human rights organizations he found particularly troubling. Soon, legislation that silenced organizations would be pushed through, his bristling given legal gravity.

Sotheary had drawn a conclusion that would have fit nicely into the new version of the *Chbap Srei* we had just finished writing: "If they come to help it's OK, but if you come to destroy my country? You can't come." She laughed, the idea that she would ever hold such power ridiculous to her. "I can't stop them but my education or my government could find the solution."

Yet she hadn't touched on my biggest area of discomfort as a white person in Cambodia. I wasn't sure how to bring it up with her. She was very innocent, and I didn't want to mar that.

"Do you…" I started. "What do you think about some of the problems that tourists here cause?"

"Oh," she said. She got what I meant. "Including the drunk or the sex tourism. Yes. We just thought about the sexual trafficking. The sexual problem in Cambodia is not only from the foreigner. It's also the people in Cambodia, too. But it's because an education. Children that are all young, they don't have education, so it's easy for the old people or the bad people came and persuade them to take money and then take them to other. It make the sexual trafficking. Especially for children, the woman, the young girl, and also from watching TV. It's not like they sell sell people from one to one, but the boy or the man that watch the sexual movie have a feeling and can't control themselves. So we have the sexual problem in some province in Cambodia, too," she said. "In my province, they have like maybe not sexual trafficking, but they love the girls and the girl didn't love him but he rape and kill her." She felt sexual assault to be a secondary effect of globalization, and newspapers were spinning it that way, too. They argued that the availability of foreign porn was to blame for an increase in rape in the country, but the particular region from which the offensive material came tended to shift with trade negotiations: Thai and Korean films were named almost interchangeably. And while it may have been true that sex trafficking was healthiest in the provinces, I had seen a lot of Western men in the country treating a lot of Khmer women poorly, in public. On the other hand, I had also met some sex workers who were perfectly happy to have escaped factory life, so it was certainly more complicated than anyone had yet described.

Some weren't even trying: sex trafficking was about to become Cambodia's *cause célèbre*, with millions of dollars in foreign aid flowing into the country to stop it, even though no real data on the practice had been compiled.

Despite her misgivings about globalization, Sotheary felt it was also supporting educational opportunities. "Like before, the girl living in Cambodia, they don't have time to study or something. But now they have the time. They can go to anywhere to go study, in the city center or in the province at the school. So I hope the women of Cambodia will think about their studying. They can achieve their goal by studying. They can do like the man. I hope they can travel around the world like you—" she giggled, because to her it was still unthinkable "—and come to Cambodia and I hope I can come to the United States."

We were now just a few weeks away from when I was to leave Cambodia and talk of my future return had started in earnest. I had also offered the alternative: That they come visit me. They loved the idea.

"Like, I saw the young girl in Phnom Penh now, they go to school but they don't think too much about study because it's like the globalization? It's not that bad, but you can see a young girl in Cambodia in the shorts, the short skirt, the clothes. And play a lot. Not study. I hope that they'll think about literature. They can do anything but don't forget about studying. Because studying is very important for themselves, for their social and for the country." The availability of cheap things made around the world was a distraction from education, and providing a new frivolous model of behavior for young women.

"Where do you think they're getting money to buy sexy clothes?" I asked.

"Most of them are in the rich family. And sometimes they wear the sexy clothes, but that doesn't mean they're from the rich family. Maybe they are in a club so that they have some sexy clothes." Worked in a nightclub, she meant. Perhaps they were waitresses, but my young friend might not know how frequently that meant they were also involved in the informal sex industry. Maybe they weren't even aware of it themselves, in truth, but a recent study had found that around half the women employed as beer promoters in Siem Reap supplemented their wages by selling sex.

"It's not traditional culture," Sotheary concluded of sexily dressed young women. "At home it's OK if they wear that." When they went out, however, Sotheary wanted them to respect their culture. "I hope they think about it," she added. "They are Cambodian."

8

FIELD TRIP

I Am Very Exciting
We were in the back of a tuk-tuk going to the Killing Fields Memorial, or *Cheung Eck* in Khmer. I had already been there, but the thirty-two Cambodians I lived with had not. They had asked me to bring them. I did not really want to, but I was not in the habit of denying them anything.

"When did you first hear about it?" I asked Dina Sun. She had been the most demanding that I escort them to this awful place.

"I first hear you will go there with me," she said. "I was very exciting. I want to see everything at *Cheung Eck.*"

In the end, only six girls wanted to go along. The rest decided they did not want to see. Dina Sun, and her morose intelligent intensity. Dara, with whom I rarely spoke, only hugged. Kimlong, who was bright and charming and never failed to smile wickedly, at anything. My roommate, Lili, who I was personally thankful would accompany us. Sunny Sotheary. And Botum. Beautiful. Quiet. Thoughtful.

Dina Sun was one of the few Cambodians in the dorm when I first arrived that had heard of the Killing Fields. Pol Pot. The Khmer Rouge. The rest needed to ask their parents, to gather information and build a portrait of what they thought the past was like. But Dina Sun's temperament, difficult as it may have been at times, allowed her to welcome the information earlier. I'd been developing a theory because of it, that the primary reason Cambodians weren't necessarily interested in the in-preparation Khmer Rouge tribunals was because it wasn't in their sunny dispositions to think bad things of each other. It's more or less what people in the provinces answered when reporters asked them how they felt about the tribunals, so my theory wasn't very interesting. Still, I found it remarkable. We don't prize *thinking nice things about each other* in the States.

"I want to know what happened there. I want to see the proof about the Khmer Rouge," Dina Sun broke off laughing at her own English. "What about you?" She turned to Sotheary.

The mood in the tuk-tuk was gay, and Sotheary was laughing and giggling in the early morning sun. It hadn't gotten hot yet, but it would, and by that point we hoped to be heading home again.

"I have heard from my mother about *Cheung Eck*," Sotheary said.

"Has she come to visit?" I asked.

"No, but she live in Pol Pot time. I have heard from her what happened then. And *Cheung Eck* have a lot of—" she broke off laughing. Most conversations with Sotheary devolved into peals of giggles at some point or another. I did not expect one about mass killing to go any differently. "*Cheung Eck*, it have a lot of ghost!" She laughed again. "And a lot of history of Pol Pot time. I am very happy to go there."

Kimlong perked up. "I just heard from Botum that we go. She tell me that it have a lot of spoons."

"Oh?" I said. She looked too serious to mean spoons. Plus I hadn't seen any on my first trip. "Skulls?" I suggested hesitantly. I had to silently vow not to use the word *skull* from then on whenever I was eating soup.

"Skull!" She repeated. "And it have a lot of prison. I just only hear only this. She tell me when we come here, I will feel so sad and so sorry about this regime. She didn't believe this regime happened, but when she come here, she understand."

"But," Sotheary added. "I am very sorry about what happened in this time. You know, I have two uncles that died during that time. They became sick and there was not medicine. Because, do you know about Pol Pot? It was very difficult. And my mother, she work very hard. A lot. And she very tired. And she don't want to do. At night, she work, and at the day, she work too. The Pol Pot time very difficult," she added. "I am very sorry."

Dina Sun and Sotheary told each other stories from their families during the Khmer Rouge time, in English. They were practicing language skills, but also the expression of grief.

•   •   •

Arrive

"Sub. Urb!" Dina Sun pointed out to me as we passed several fields and nicer houses in a quiet part of town. We were nearly at *Cheung Eck*. She was right. We were in a suburb. "There is a lot of fresh air," she added, grabbing the microphone like the hostess of a TV talk show. "And the view is so beautiful. I like it so much." I flashed on what Cambodian newscasts would be like if young Khmer women really genuinely reported on what was happening in the world from their perspective. "Everything is great again today!" would be the lead story in every newscast. Thus Khmer Teen News TV would probably be very boring, although I would still watch every episode.

"The foreigner have to buy a ticket," Dina Sun noted as we pulled in through the gate that acts as the entry way to the memorial.

"Yes," I said, and walked up to the ticket desk. "One," I told the guard in Khmer. He glanced at the five young women tittering behind me. "They are Khmer," I explained, because Cambodians visit for free.

"Oh!" He acted surprised, although he probably could have guessed it. "We do not have many Khmer people here," he said in English.

"*Akun*," I said, and went to rejoin my girls.

Of course they thought the way I said *Thank you* was hilarious.

.   .   .

Stupa

A massive Stupa greets visitors to *Cheung Eck*, a tall white thing where you leave your shoes, pick up some incense to burn, and then go in to visit stacks and stacks and stacks of skulls. Many have signs that describe the person who used to own the skull: *JUVENILE FEMALE KAMPUCHEAN from 15 to 20 years old*, read one. And another: *ADULT MALE KAMPUCHEAN from 35 to 40 years old.*

A bit of recorded chaipei music wafted from a boombox in the corner of the Stupa. My girls went suddenly and completely quiet.

I'd never seen them like that before. "Do you want to describe for me what we're looking at?" I asked Sotheary and Kimlong, who stood together peering at the skull of a young woman who had been about their age, thirty years ago, when she was killed by other Cambodians somewhere nearby where we now stood.

"It have a lot of skulls of people that died in the Pol Pot regime," Sotheary said. She counted. "Sixteen level of skulls," she announced, looking up at the very top glass shelf of human remains. "Each one full of skulls." Under the shelves were clothes, torn and dug up with the bodies, a mass of cloth. "They wore these," she added.

"We have to dye all our clothes," Dina Sun explained, referring to the Khmer Rouge demand that everyone wear only black. "We only have one clothes, mostly, for four year." Dye was expensive and, as everyone had been marched out to the provinces to farm rice with nothing but what they could carry, most owned only one set of clothes.

Kimlong also answered my question. "No," she said. And walked away.

•   •   •

I am Sorry, I Cannot Stop to Cry

Lili practiced her English reading me signs out loud as we tromped the quiet Killing Fields. Technically, many of them were in Khmenglish, and didn't make much sense to me, linguistically. Also, they did not make sense to me emotionally.

"Many people did not die at first, so the Khmer Rouge must pour a lye on them to poison the living and cover the smell of the bodies for the neighbors," Lili read to me. "Sister? Is it right? How I say?"

She had pronounced all of the words correctly, yes. *Is it right?* I repeated in my mind. No. It was atrocious, in act as well as in representation. There are not conditions under which one *must* pour a lye on living people. How was I to explain? *How I say?* I wanted to ask her. Of course I speak English, but I do not know how to explain what the English means in this situation, really, or what happened here over three decades ago. I was a child, 5, when the Khmer Rouge regime ousted the American-backed Lon Nol and began its brutal rule of Cambodia. I was eight thousand miles away.

"Here was the place where victims were transported from Tuoul Sleng and another place in the country. Usually when the trucks arrived the victims were execute—ex – ah – cute—" she stumbled a bit.

"Executed," I offered. Kindly. As kindly as one can.

"Executed," Lili repeated.

"Good," I said, absurdly.

"*Executed immediately. However, as the numbers grew to over 300 per day, the execut—executer. Ex – ah – cu – shun—*"

"Executioner," Kimlong stepped in. Her smile was gone. What she was doing with her mouth was called frowning. I had not seen it in the dorm before.

Lili looked at me expectantly.

"Executioner," I agreed. It was only an English lesson, I silently noted. "Do you know what that is?"

"Killer," Kimlong said flatly.

"Kill-ar," Lili repeated in her less-than-steady accent.

Kimlong mumbled something quick in Khmer to Lili and Lili quickly looked back at the sign in horror. "He is Cambodian," she said to me. Meaning: the executioner was one of them.

We were standing in front of the detention center, where the Khmer Rouge held overflow live bodies it had deemed necessary to kill. About a year into the regime, there was no longer time for the shoestring operation to physically meet the demands of killing its enemies; sometimes the killings had to be put off for 24 hours. Around that same time, rice had become scarce. *Angkar* was using it to send back to China to pay off debts, and people had started to become nervous: How long was this revolution going to take? Workers were dying of starvation, and meals had dwindled from three to two, sometimes one per day. Sometimes only a few grains of rice in each bowl of watery soup. No protein for weeks at a time, or longer. Some grew accustomed to foraging—bugs, what animals they could find and secretly prepare. More and more were killed for insurrection, and whether or not this meant in individual cases that more were insurrecting or that *Angkar* was just getting paranoid will never be known. Likely both.

What is known is that Brother Number Two, Nuon Chea, claims there was no violence. "Ours was a peaceful regime," he has been known to confide in supporters. He has also made clear that, to the regime, there were only two threats to Khmer national security: the Americans and the Vietnamese. Where he gets less clear is regarding how the regime differentiated between Cambodians who had an American influence and those who had a Vietnamese one. In fact, he has even been unclear on how to tell Vietnamese from Cambodians, a distinction largely irrelevant along that border anyway. Mistakes may have been made, Nuon Chea has acknowledged. He hasn't admitted to any, but sometimes, he has said, they do happen.

The truth is that the majority of those killed under the Khmer Rouge regime were the same race, ethnicity, and religion as the killers. Reporter Thet Sambath and film producer Rob Lemkin released a documentary called *Enemies of the People* in 2010 in which they tracked down Nuon Chea and asked him what happened. As the tribunal was getting underway in 2008, this ambivalence about the ethnicity of those killed would have legal repercussions. Genocide, by definition, can only be perpetrated against others, whether a significant fraction of a population has been destroyed or not. Sambath's own paper, the *Phnom Penh Post*, published figures in late 2010 that suggested around eighteen point seven percent of the ethnic Khmer population alive at the time perished under the Khmer Rouge.

To me, it was horrifying that deaths in such mass quantities and under such circumstances could have happened at all. However what terrified the girls was that Cambodians had committed them against other Cambodians.

Sure, they giggled when they could not find the correct word, or over their mispronunciations, or because that is just what young women do. But it was not very funny, deep inside.

•   •   •

Chemical Storage Room
"*Here was the place where chemical substances such as DDT, etc., was kept. Executioners scattered these substances over dead bodies of the victims at once after execution. This action had two purposes. Firstly, to eliminate the stench from the dead bodies which could potentially raise suspicion among people working nearby the Killing Fields, and secondly was to kill off victims who were buried alive,*" Lili read to me.

We could see houses from where we stood. Just see them, they were over there. It is probably one thing to commit a grand-scale atrocity such as murdering well over a million and a half people, but it seems like it must be another to do it quietly, so the neighbors can pretend it is not happening and continue working in their fields.

Cheung Eck was calm the day we visited. Kimlong enjoyed the peacefulness. "It is very good to keep quiet in this place," she said.

Lili broke in: "But, my friend told me about this tree, that it become very loud here at night. They have a player—" she meant a boombox, and the mid-1970s version that came immediately to mind was a monster of a thing, black, with two big blaring speakers—"and they put it in the tree and it play, at night. So no one hear about their ... party."

Lili's English was less steady than Kimlong's, but she didn't overthink her sentences in the rush to communicate, instead spitting out words in her Wild West manner to build an immediate approximation of what she wanted to convey. It was clear that she meant, *loud gathering of people*, and not, you know, *party*, but she went on to describe the festivities in detail so I would understand.

We found the tree she was referring to, and next to it was a sign. *Magic Tree: The tree was used as a tool to hang a loudspeaker which make sound louder to avoid moan of victims while they are being executed.*

"They put a thing over the eye," she explained to me.

"A blindfold?" I pantomimed it.

"Blindfold. And then they stand over there, and *Pshew! Pshew!* To kill them."

"Shot them," I said.

"Yeah," she agreed.

Unfortunately, she was wrong. Ammunition, about a year in, became too precious to use for any purposes other than defending against possible raids from the Vietnamese, or whoever else might be planning an attack. People were instead killed intimately, with hunting knives, or sharp pieces of bamboo. The necessity of poisoning those buried alive was, simply but horridly, because the *Angkar's* improvised methods of killing were not very sure.

The tree was a massive, beautiful thing with a deep dark stain, slightly higher than where we stood. "It is where the soldier take the children," Lili said. "And smash."

. . .

Feel Scare

Dara had been quite quiet.

"Because I have not before seen," Dara told me, "I feel scare."

"Do you feel scared now?" I asked her, more as a translation issue than to check in, emotionally.

"Yes," she said. And threw both arms around me, burying her head in my shoulder.

"Oh Dara," I said. "I wish I knew how to protect you."

Dina Sun spotted the hug and joined in.

"Because I am Cambodian," she said, "I feel so very sad. And maybe you don't understand about my feelings. I am Khmer." She was almost accusatory. She had a right to be. I could make no claim to understand it either. "How Pol Pot can do it? How can he? I no understand," she said. At least her confusion I could share in.

We were on a small dirt path, next to a clearing that had not yet been excavated. We broke from our group hug, but remained close, holding hands. I spotted a shard of bone poking out of the ground, a femur. I didn't mention it.

"Why do you think Cambodians do not come here?" I asked them.

Dina Sun replied. "I think maybe they want to come here, but they do not know. Maybe they think it too expensive, to come. They cannot afford to travel. They have no time. But sometimes I think they do not want to come here, because this place remind them how difficult they have made, during that time."

We continued on our walk, wandering by mass graves, still being dug up. Signs marked the number of victims found. Heads were sometimes buried separately from bodies. The numbers didn't always add up, and Sotheary found this particularly distressing.

Eventually the girls stopped cataloguing individual horrors and took the experience in as a whole. Birds twittered in the trees, children played off in the distance.

450, Lili pointed to the sign. The number of headless bodies found in one mass grave. Her eyes got big. "I scare of ghost," she confessed. Then laughed, gaily, at her own adorable loving girlhood, as we moved on to the next site.

A few feet ahead of me, a dusty bit of black cloth, becoming unburied with each passing footstep. *There are bodies where I stand*, I thought, not wanting to say it out loud. Just thinking it. *There are bodies where I stand.*

•   •   •

Profit

"What do you think about the company that runs this place?" I asked them.

"I happy," Sotheary explained. "That so many foreigner want to come here to learn the truth about Cambodia. I thankful for them."

Tourists poured through the doors of the entrance we could see across the field. Because I was with Cambodians, they clustered, leaving me and the Euglossa team a respectful distance ahead of them. You could see that they were curious. Several hundred foreign tourist dollars had passed hands since we had arrived.

"Do you know it is a Japanese company?" I asked.

"A Japanese company?" Sotheary repeated. "Why they care?"

"Tourism," Kimlong said without looking up from the ground. "They get to keep the money."

"When I am leader, I will make it change," Sotheary said. "I want to develop Cambodia, but I want to develop it for Cambodians."

•   •   •

The Exact Number of Sads

Next to each marked attraction, a small gold Buddha's house. People used them to stack bones they would find as they wandered, the flip flops of the dead.

Kimlong, who had been lagging behind, caught up to me, bent over the ground, staring at the smooth face of another bone encased in dirt. Her eyes calculated.

"Oh," she said.

"In my mind, I don't know how to describe it, how to show it," Dina Sun said from behind us, approaching. She giggled.

"I only know I can say sorry," Sotheary said. "I very very sorry." She said it gravely. "Sad sad sad sad sad—"

I cut her off. (I rarely did that.) "Four hundred sads?" I inquired.

She laughed openly. "No, more."

"Five hundred?"

"Unlimited," she over-pronounced each syllable. *Un. Lim. I. Ted.* "Unlimited sads."

•   •   •

Scale

The more time we spent there, the more the girls committed lapses in language: *They,* to refer to the murderers became *he*—Pol Pot. *We,* which meant Cambodians under normal circumstances, now meant *the younger generation of Cambodian.* Maybe even: *Girl Cambodians.* And *sad* meant: Deeply confused. Shocked. Sorrowful. Without comprehension.

"What about your feeling?" Lili asked me as we stood in front of a sign that pointed out where a hundred bodies had been discovered. A small roof overhung the area.

"My feeling is also sad, and confused," I told her. I looked at the mass grave. "How big is this space, do you think. As big as our bedroom?"

"No," she said. "Not so big."

A tightly compressed sorrow, then. I wondered how often it lapsed into other emotions: Unexplained fear, boundless rage, everlasting love. They all felt proximal, then.

•   •   •

An Ugly Place

"Some of the people that still live from Pol Pot regime, they think that, if Pol Pot still alive, they will kill him," Dina Sun said morosely.

"And cut him," added Kimlong. Point of fact.

"Hit and kick," Sotheary added. A regular pile on.

"Kill, cut, hit, and kick," I said. "But what do you think about, that he was not the only person. It was not only his fault, it was many people. What do you think about the tribunal that will start this year, about holding others responsible?"

"Pol Pot is the leader," Dina Sun explained.

"Yes, but people are still angry. And he is already dead," I prompted.

"Pol Pot is the leader," she repeated.

We left the memorial area. Within a few years a fancy new building would be created, with a theater and displays. None of this existed yet. Everything was raw and powerful. When the new buildings would be installed, more tourists would come, more complaints about the cleanliness of grounds. It would get busier, soon, and louder, but this moment, with these young women who'd asked me to help them explore their own past, would soon be over. Soon time for quiet sharing like this would become impossible in the hustle and bustle of their future. I felt deeply sad then, not for their history, or for the drastic barriers they would need to surmount to overcome it, but that the time we had together to prepare for it was ending.

We walked to the exit and found our driver, a kind man who enjoyed a good nap, and roused him for our return, plying him with cold sodas if not good cheer.

"What did you think?" I asked Lili as we pulled away in the tuk-tuk. We were intimate like secret conspirators. She put a hand on my knee, about to become serious. It was a forgiving gesture of enormous grace.

"It so pretty," she said. "But it an ugly place."

9

Nobody Miss You

I Do Not Want You Home
Dara had very dark skin and thick eyebrows like mine, not the discrete ones most Southeast Asian women had. We always had a language problem, although not a communication problem, so when we interacted it was very visual. Or hug-based.

I had taken the girls on a boat trip along the Mekong River because it was a popular way to celebrate and many of them had not yet been. We rented a boat and brought food and were expected to have enough to offer the captain and his crew, and in fact they ate quite a bit so that is something to keep in mind if you ever want to rent a boat along the Mekong. Additionally, a feature the boats were excited to offer at the time was that they could play a CD you had brought with you, even though it was expected that you would want to play the same basic twenty-five songs everyone else in the country was already familiar with, although the fact that you could play them in a new order was probably an enticement. I had devised an alternative plan. After Jorani had quizzed me about the meaning of punk I made a mix CD that explored gender and low-budget cultural production. These songs would probably never have ended up on a local karaoke playlist, so I brought the mix on the boat trip. It went over OK. Not great. We danced a lot, and only one young woman asked if I really liked this kind of music.

I accepted with resignation that my musical education efforts had been proven a failure when Dara came in to my room to ask if she could borrow the CD to exercise. By this she meant, _hula hoop_. I grabbed it for her; I had everything I owned in neat stacks anyway. I was packing to leave.

"Sister, where, where, are you go today." She said things, quietly, instead of asking them. Rather, she was so unsure of her language abilities that everything sounded like a question, every word, and the uplift at the end of the last one was no different from that at the end of the first. It was easier to think of it all as an expression of her permanent state of wonderment at the world than it was to feel interrogated all the time. Sometimes I asked her to speak in Khmer, when she became a different person. Confident, sharp, and quick. Yet one I could not understand.

"Dara, I do not go today. I pack to go home Friday. *Khnyom tdao phtas.* I do not know the days of the week." I explained this in English, although she probably did not have the vocabulary to understand what I said. Anyway, it was true, I did not know the days of the week, because that would imply I could also communicate matters related to a time different than *Now.* I did, however, know which colors to wear to experience the most luck on any given day. Dara herself had shown me, in a laughing but mostly wordless tour of her closet.

"Sister." She started crying. "I do not want you home."

"I know, Dara. Me either." I would be in Cambodia for four more days. They looked to be tearful for all of us.

·   ·   ·

When You are Boring
The goodbyes began in earnest then, as well as the preparations for my return home. I had my last Khmer language lesson, which of all of them was perhaps the biggest joke, because I hadn't been able to think in English, much less Khmer, for an entire week.

I drew up a list of things I would not miss:

GRODY WHITE DUDES IN MASSES I HAVE NEVER BEFORE EXPERIENCED REALLY EXPLORING THEIR DISGUSTING NATURES IN PUBLIC

DIARRHEA

THAT SOMETIMES NOTHING AT ALL WORKS, FOR DAYS, INCLUDING ELECTRICITY AND WEATHER AND STOMACHS

THE DEAD BLANK STARE OF POLICE OFFICERS AND OTHER AUTHORITY FIGURES

SOME OF THE SMELLS. MOST OF THE SMELLS.

A nostalgic family of termites moved in to my laptop. The picture on my desktop, which was of some raw chicken soaking in milk that I found beautiful, disgusted the girls, who asked me to change it. I did, to a picture of all the students, standing there on the boat, looking contentedly into the camera. They looked happy and excited and maybe a little bit tired from dancing. I have the picture now, on a wall behind my desk as I type this. Two of the girls are holding small zines in their hands, trades from earlier in the day. Those are zines I never read. I have no idea what they are about. Zines were just a part of girl culture by then.

"Only one more day," Amoun said. She came in and watched while I packed. "One more day where you can hear my voice."

"Yes," I told her. She had an exam later. I wished her good luck on it. "And today, if you have a hard time on your exam, you just think, *Anne*. It will not help you, but it will be nice or me!"

"Yes." She said. "And when you are at home and you are boring, you must think: *Amoun*."

. . .

Nobody Think of You
I had received a mysterious text message at some point, which I had assumed was from some kind of spam service, or a product of some other shady deal I didn't want to know too much about. My cell phone received a lot of texts from radio stations, from randoms who wanted to know who I was and if I was happy, from the cell phone company itself. I'd met a man at Angkor Wat who introduced me to his girlfriend, who was visiting both him and the temple for the first time.

"Until this day, we only know each other by phone," he said.

And I wondered: How does that work? Did you missed call to her? Did you text random people until some girl wrote you back? Did you take the numbers from a friend's phone? Did someone set you up? Are you confuse? It didn't matter. They seemed perfectly content together.

This was the message I received, mysterious but delightful:
Hi.
Nobody think of you.
Nobody miss you.
Nobody want to know who are you?
I am is Nobody.

I had kept it on my phone as a pondering tool, a digital Buddhist koan, until one day I showed it to Botum.

"It from the dorm," she said simply.

So several weeks after I had received it I asked Sotheary, one of the smartest and cleverest and silliest girls in the dorm: "Hey, did you send me this creepy but very, very clever message?"

She said she did. "I think you receive it and think sad, *Oh nobody think of me? Nobody miss me?*" She said. "*Nobody want to know who am I? Well, I am is Nobody,*" she told me. "*I think of you. I miss you. I want to know who are you.*"

It was a silly romantic gesture, and I was deeply moved by it. It didn't make any sense at all if you looked at it with your eyes, of course. You had to close them, and look only with your heart. It was exactly how I had come to think of Cambodia.

•   •   •

Hot Dogs for Thirty Two

Not wanting to leave the girls with nothing to remember me by save the questionable value of the high five, I made them all hot dogs my last night in town. I lectured extensively on the evils of ketchup to give them the true Chicago experience. (Ketchup they always claimed to be a quintessential American food. This was a belief couched in the understanding that Americans eating tomatoes as if they were vegetables is *crazy*, since they were clearly a *dessert*, and I tried to impress upon them that it is the sweetness of the tomato that makes ketchup such a bad topping for a Chicago-style hot dog. Among these young women, anything in a plastic squeeze bottle holds the irresistible allure of a science project that has perhaps gone poorly. My lecture on ketchup was surprisingly detailed, complex, and perhaps the harshest and most critical set of statements I had yet visited upon these young women, and I was surprised to discover that they were *fascinated* by it.)

I substituted various Cambodian sauces of lime, chili, fish paste, and whatever else they felt *was probably exactly like ketchup*, since their primary purpose was not to experience the hot dog, but to be seen experiencing the hot dog, to be photographed in the process of eating a hot dog. They felt, as is only right, probably, that the taste of the hot dog would be wan if not appalling; they were not interested in it as a food item so much as they felt it was an induction into The American Experience.

Only Jorani heeded my advice and ate hers with mustard exclusively; Sotheary, Dara, and a host of others found the volume and consistency of bread paired with meat distressing and threw the bun out. Many photographs were taken; most had girls smiling hard, holding up the hot dog and two fingers, no real intention to consume it, just to show. Branding themselves. Ready for their future.

Later, they made rice, a secret addendum to the meal. Perhaps, a correction.

•   •   •

What Girls in Cambodia Do For Fun
I drafted a layout of *New Girl Law*. I drew it up by hand and thought through how I wanted it to look, what kind of a book would both impress them but also be clearly their own. I showed the layout to everyone in a meeting late one night after dinner in the chicken when they all, miraculously, happened to be on a simultaneous study break, probably due to my pending departure. Even Ms. Channy stopped by, far after she should have returned home, to murmur approval at the layout. They liked it. They decided that they wanted a picture of themselves in their school uniforms for the back cover, and there wasn't one with everyone. I agreed to take a new one if they would agree to be ready for it at 6 a.m. before my flight. And, you know what? Every single girl was there. Freshly pressed, clean and tidy, stunningly beautiful, without complaint.

So that's how I woke up the morning I left Cambodia. Taking a picture of thirty-two professionally dressed young Khmer women leaders, a visual representation of the new girl order for the inside cover of a book they'd written to tell you all about it.

•   •   •

Last Tuk-tuk Ride

It's one of the great pleasures of Cambodia and the only one I don't really fault tourists for taking full advantage of at every opportunity: Riding around in a little wheeled cart, the whole thing to yourself, driven about by a nimble motorcycle at the fore. Really it is quite nice. It is hard to do without spreading out, all over the back, arms out to either side tucked about the top of the seat as if you owned the thing, as if you had two imaginary girlfriends and you were a slicked-back hair dude from 1957 in a Camaro. A good breeze will build up in no time, and you are already in the shade. There just isn't a better way to travel. The adventure of a motorcycle, the comfort of a well-paced convertible, no navigational stress.

So this was my planned mode of transport to the plane, my last hurrah, and I was ready for it. Except then five slim Khmer girls climbed in next to me: Chandara, Ryna, Kimlong, Botum, and Maly. So, last minute change to my naively crafted plan, we all went to the airport together. Singing, mostly, and telling stories, and making jokes about which suitcase I could still fit them into, if they wanted to come with. The truth was: I couldn't fit them. Every available inch I'd carefully carved out for souvenirs was instead filled with zines, the small gifts I'd purchased for folks back home earlier entrusted to the Cambodian postal service, the last I ever saw of them. The young women cried some, or were quiet. Perhaps the best part, unforeseen: I got to throw my arms over the backs of both sides of the seat, no imagination necessary, a girl snuggled into each one.

I didn't cry. Not because I wasn't deeply, deeply sad to be leaving but for reasons I did not tell the girls, that I couldn't possibly have explained to them. That I had spent the last year crying: The death of my father, the end of a career in independent print magazine publishing, the loss of all friendships that went with that. The loss of community. I had given away so much in the last year, and I couldn't shed tears in a situation in which I had only gained. Instead I was silent, and this was unusual enough to attract attention.

"You're not crying," each noted at different times. "Because you are strong. But you will miss us. We know."

"No." They have a tendency to perceive in me only positive traits, to interpret all my actions in the best possible light. "It's not because I am strong. It's because I will miss you too much to cry. It's because every minute

I could spend crying would be better spent trying to plan my next trip. Or trying to make sure you have the opportunity to come visit me."

I didn't tell them: *Some of you have very serious medical conditions that endanger your lives. Some of you will probably be involved in a traffic accident. Some of you will raise your voice, be reprimanded, and never do it again. Some of you will marry and become housewives. Some of you will have babies, and no longer speak in English. Some of you will find this life of change too hard, and retreat. Some of you will receive scholarships to the United States and be rewarded for your success not on Cambodian terms but on American ones, and you will leave your homeland for mine, but we will no longer value the same things. Some of you will succumb, finally, to the intense peer pressure that besets all young Cambodian women, and capitulate, remaining quiet and steady, but you will be deeply unhappy. As much as I love you, I don't know how to help you get through any of that. So I will not waste my time crying right now. I have too much to do.*

Epilogue

Winter hadn't quite ended by the time I got back to Chicago, and in the spring I did a residency at an arts organization where I studied binding and printing techniques with a group of extremely talented book-makers. I letter-pressed the pages of *New Girl Law* at that time, although was only able to bind one copy (of the fifty I had prepared) by June. Completing the rest took me the remaining months of 2008.

During the residency, with my young collaborators' permission, I also created an audio version of the book, selections from the conversations that had lead to the final rules included in *New Girl Law*. The occasionally intense discussions, many transcribed here, held interesting clues as to what young women undergoing a rapid process of globalization felt wasn't being addressed as their country developed economically. I also felt the physical object of the book required a clear connection to its creation process, if people who hadn't been involved in writing it were to comprehend its intent. The book would be viewed in art environments, a context that minimizes social and cultural relevance. It seemed the smartest solution to have the creators provide elaboration in their own voices.

The organization where I did my residency was founded on principles of free expression, a space supposedly devoted to curator- and editor-free creative exploration. No boundaries, no censorship, no restrictions. I did, however, require assistance. I hoped to broadcast the audio online, so my young friends in the dorm—with a special top-secret link, a password, and other security barriers—could hear it for themselves. These preparations took some finagling. A fantastic team of tech enthusiasts and I, after much experimentation, crafted a way of streaming audio as safely as possible. To further ensure my collaborators' privacy, we included no markers of their identities.

A few nights before my residency ended, I gave a talk on the project. The audio was to stream the next day, so I played excerpts, showed off the book, and described the process of creating it. I also showed the zines the Euglossa girls had made, and talked openly and seriously about how stifling censorship was on young women who barely felt free to express themselves *about cute boys*, much less about an emerging economy that didn't value their input. What was made clear by the zines, however, was that offering young women the chance to express their concerns—really ensuring them freedom of speech—resulted in narratives that were loving, supportive, caring, and invested. Intelligent, certainly. But far from critical. This was also the point made by the audio piece: That what young women wanted from democracy was the chance to express more joy.

I packed and prepared to leave town. Then I was informed that broadcast of the audio had been cancelled by the director of the organization, a man who had otherwise expressed enthusiasm for the project. There had been no discussion or explanation. The audio hadn't even been reviewed first, nor had any of the tech folks been consulted. And no one would meet with me to discuss the matter. The voices of young women in a developing nation were simply silenced. Again.

I spent some months considering the matter. These were also the months that the economy crashed, and jobs and financial security all took a heavy hit around the world. The global garment trade, tourism. Cambodia's biggest money-earners. Support for my own work. My emotions, too. I wanted to return to Cambodia, but funding was unavailable. So during November and December of 2008, I finished binding all copies of the book *New Girl Law*. It was beautiful, a gold silk-covered hardback square volume with gold and black letterpress printing. Inside: a picture of all the young women in the dorm, in their school uniforms, radiant and smart. I felt it was worthy of its creators, of who they were becoming.

Caroline, who'd first introduced me to Euglossa, was returning to Phnom Penh shortly before Christmas, and I sent four copies along with her. I was touchy about the books: I only wanted to send four, in case there were any concerns about safety. I wanted the volumes to remain well concealed, and be delivered to the dorm, and only to the dorm. Once there, I didn't want them to leave. Four books, I reasoned, would be enough. One for each of the three floors' libraries and one for the dorm manager's office, so Ms. Sonrith Channy could show off some of the guiding principles of the new generation of emerging women leaders. Caroline understood my concerns, and was kind to honor them. She'd spent more time in Cambodia than I had, however, and didn't share them. She seemed to think it would be fine.

When Caroline returned to Chicago after her trip, she showed me pictures of the young women receiving the golden books they had written together. There was also an audio recording of them opening the box I had stored the books in. When Caroline told them it had come from me, there was some bickering about what might be inside. Eventually they agreed it must be candy. Their enthusiasm is evident, too, in the photographs. There they are, young women, slightly older and more mature than when I saw them last, eagerly pawing gold documents we had created together. The audio switches to wonderment when they find the books instead of sweets. They proudly show off their creation to the visiting Americans, for Caroline has brought some people along to the dorm. Ryna reads aloud to them, excitedly explaining how long it took to write these rules, trilling her words to get them all out in a rush. Amoun comments on the books' beauty; even Dara offers a shy, "It nice."

The photographs show them appreciating it. You could almost perceive a sense of wonder and trust growing in their eyes. It's not always the case that foreigners keep promises to Cambodians; it's not always the case that Americans keep promises to anyone.

They're hard pictures for me to look at, however. Even before I had seen them, or heard for myself the young women's excitement over the books, I had received an angry email from the dorm manager. Ms. Sonrith Channy wrote me in the early days of 2009 that the books I had sent had been destroyed, because it is dangerous to criticize the government. She asked why I had ever bothered to make them at all. She said I was a dangerous person to have around young women in Cambodia.

And yes, there in the background of several of the photographs, you could see Ms. Channy, glaring at the book she had once called important.

•   •   •

Ms. Sonrith Channy left the dorm shortly thereafter; I never understood her anger, especially given her previous support. Perhaps she had been counting on the book never seeing the light of day, or had never understood its purpose. It didn't matter. Sometimes, in truth, this is how working with survivors of trauma goes.

I also never understood the degree to which her anger spread among the young women of Euglossa. I never brought it up to them, although we have remained reasonably close over the years. To a degree, this didn't matter either: I was the non-leader among them. I had no intention to push through any sort of American feminist agenda. I only wanted to support young Cambodian women's struggles for their own rights. From the beginning, it was a process they had led, and one I made no claims to understand as well as they did.

Still, the intention when Ryna first suggested the project had been to identify deeply embedded, long-standing fears of self-expression for young women nudged toward silence by the *Chbap Srei*. The outcome of this inquiry had then been silenced, on two continents, by parties who presumably felt the need to step in and offer protection. This was becoming a popular approach to transnational solidarity around women's issues in Cambodia. Nick Kristof at the *New York Times* shortly thereafter took this approach to entirely new levels in his rush to save Khmer young women. Brothel raids he began conducting with Cambodian activist Somaly Mam were presented as freeing forced sex workers from enslavement. In fact, some of these young women later complained that the armed guards and locked doors that protected them once freed merely kept them from jobs they worked willingly—one of few opportunities for women in the country to earn a living wage. This isn't an injustice Kristof acknowledges, however, and I can't help but see a connection between his disinterest in allowing this truth expression and the recognition he receives for being a savior.

In other words, we seem willing to overlook silencing when it's presented as protection. But unwilling to acknowledge that it is still censorship.

•　　　•　　　•

On the other hand, there is more to be considered.

New Girl Law was a project that embraced a particularly Western feminist approach to social change, one first given form in 1848 when Elizabeth Cady Stanton and other folks drafted the Declaration of Sentiments and then gathered in Seneca Falls, New York to present it to the public. The demands this document forwarded included the right to vote, the right to own property, the right to profitable employment, and the right to education. It took seventy-two years for the first of these to be achieved, and another ninety-two, once the 19th Amendment guaranteeing women's suffrage was passed, for female voters to significantly sway an election. In the U.S. in 2012, women—appalled by losses to reproductive rights in particular—finally exerted political force to be reckoned with, both at the polls and on the ballot: The 113th Congress, being sworn in even as I write, holds a record twenty percent female senators and eighteen percent women in the House of Representatives. American feminists celebrated.

Other areas of concern to Western feminists have seen less progress—or none. When the 19th Amendment was passed in 1920, to calls that women's access to the polls would end child labor, slightly over a hundred and thirty-four thousand minors were working in conditions deemed, by the passage of the 1938 Fair Labor Standards Act, unjust and criminal. Laws now exist to protect against domestic child labor, but two million young people hold jobs in violation of them, fifteen times as many since women gained the right to vote. Women still earn approximately seventy-seven percent of what men do, an average that has stayed more or less consistent (according to the National Committee on Pay Equity) since 2005. Women of color earn significantly less. Adjusted for inflation, the closure of the wage gap has never happened faster than by a half penny per year. And even though over half the students enrolled in college in the U.S. are women, and they get slightly better grades on average, female college graduates earn about $7,600 USD less per year than male college graduates—or only eighty-two percent (according to the American Association of University Women).

Although feminists celebrated the historic gains for women in politics, in 2013 the U.S. dropped—from 72nd place in 2012 to 83rd place—in an international rank of countries in which women hold parliamentary seats (according to the Inter-Parliamentary Union).

To outsiders, that might look like failure. Afterall, in that same rank, Cambodia comes in at 69th.

•   •   •

The little gold book called *New Girl Law* can be found around Cambodia, and around Cambodian-American organizations in the U.S., and in private homes. It's served as a tool for pondering gender equity and human rights among heads of state and undocumented youth populations across the globe, and as a prompt for discussions of censorship and freedom of expression in Cambodia and the U.S. I'd like to think it's had more impact than if it had been embraced by the original thirty-two young women it was intended for, but I can't be sure. What I can say with certainty is this: To address and correct the global condition of women as an underclass throughout the world, it's going to take far more than thirty-three of us.

And I've learned two things about we will need. We will need to listen, and we will need to be patient.

When I went to Phnom Penh in 2007 after running *Punk Planet* for several years, the music of the U.S. cultural underground was still the primary way I organized the world. Even my own field, writing and publishing, sort of fit itself in around musical styles, genres, and acts—distinctions I based on matters both aesthetic and political. I like independently produced music and media, sure, but I also feel it's *important*. Now: I don't play music—I never enjoyed it, to my parents' unending chagrin. But I had been making my own booklets—zines—since I was 11, originally a solitary act that later met up with the early-1990's music and self-publishing scene. So when I was invited to do a project with the first large group of young women to attend college together in the history of Cambodia, of course I planned to show them how to make zines. And of course, to explain what zines were and could do—to young people who are taught to write via rote memorization, and who live under an oppressive regime where journalists are regularly threatened, harmed, or worse for printing facts about the government—I used music. Luckily, one of my students came across the word, *punk*. She asked me what it was in my self-publishing class—but her only familiarity with U.S. music at the time was Britney Spears. I started there.

"You know how Britney Spears mostly sings songs about boys," I told her, later recorded in chapter five of *Cambodian Grrrl*, "when really there are many other things to think about? Like cooking, or going to school, or politics? And she makes a bad role model for girls by only thinking about boys? Britney works for a big music company. That's why even though she lives in the U.S., and she has never been to Cambodia, and maybe has never even heard of it, you see pictures of her every day. A punk is someone who wants music to be different, to not be like that, so makes their own music. And maybe sings about boys, but maybe sings about politics, or cooking, or something else. And they don't just make music, they also make their own magazines, and books, and comics, and clothes."

My students were intrigued, but not satisfied. One of them asked if you had to be a boy to be a punk. Because, in Cambodia, you pretty much have to be a boy to be anything.

"Many punks are boys," I told her, "but there are punks that are girls, too. Girls that think boys get too much attention in society and want to make their own things instead of buying things boys make. They want to support each other in making girl things." I didn't tell them about riot grrrl, because they would say to me, rioting is not good. But I did make them a mix CD—something for them *to exercise to* (which meant *hula-hooping*). This was, more or less, what I put on it.

EXTRAORDINARY, LIZ PHAIR

There's a thing in Cambodia called "sweet voice," an extremely high-pitched, lyric and lilting tone that young women, by dint of the *Chbap Srei* (*Girl Law*), are urged to use. I put it first on the mix hoping the gritty driving guitar in the opening, Phair's own sweet voice, and catchy tune would cause these young women to wander around the city singing, "I am extraordinary," and that, somehow, the country would take notice.

LOVE ME OR HATE ME, LADY SOVEREIGN

That part in the middle, where she belches really loud? I think that's great. Fuck yeah, put that in your song. This is why I don't have kids.

HANG ON KIDS, GHOST MICE

I did an all-ages show once with Chris Clavin and Hannah Jones' acoustic, folksy pop-punk band, and they played this great little song on the guitar and violin. It sums up the scruffy-loser-punk experience of going to high school as well as, strangely, that of the elite corps of young women leaders of Cambodia, the first large group to be able to go to college *en masse*. The problem with the song's false promise to these young women—"if you just hang on, I swear you'll be all right"—remains that: For the first large group of women to receive college degrees, there weren't likely to be any jobs waiting for them. Most of them would probably not get married, and after college, they wouldn't find many peers. Still, you gotta get through the day somehow.

I Wish I Was Him, Kathleen Hanna

The first time I heard this song I was involved in an amazing collaborative young feminist radio project at WORT in Madison WI in 1994. I had been dating boys in bands for years, and was usually the only girl in any given room—and I worked in some pretty aggressive environments (comedy, political publishing). So after Hanna's innocent-enough guitar kicked in, and by the time she started professing deep jealousy over some dude's minor sense of privilege, I was feeling dirty and exposed. The song is honest and unencumbered, another example of sweet voice not being used to comply with what dominant culture may want, but being used to rebel against it. For me, it laid bare the pure jealousy that sometimes sat at the heart of my aggressive stance. I put it on the girls' mix, however, because it precisely mirrored the conversations I had with these young women, who wanted to work in politics or do journalism or run banks—if only they'd been born men.

Keep on the Sunny Side of Life, the Carter Family

I am not a performer by nature, but was asked to appear in a staged reading of a biographical comic adaptation David Lasky was undertaking of the Carter Family's story (should be out in a couple years). I agreed without thinking too seriously about it and was really only on stage before I pieced together that I was about to *sing. Out loud. For people.* Cartoonist Ellen Forney—the other pretend Carter sister—pretty much carried us through this song and "Chewing Gum," and I grew to love the Carter Family after that. Plus, for second-generation genocide survivors, the young women I was working with were amazingly perky, so it just sort of fit their mix, even though it's not a great hula-hooping song. Which I heard about for *weeks,* believe you me.

Ways To Save Our Lives, Holy Roman Empire

The post-hardcore act headed by killer-voiced Emily Schambra, then on Hewhocorrupts Inc., was one of the funnest shows I saw in the waning days of *Punk Planet,* shortly before I left for Southeast Asia, even though I did crack a tooth in the mosh pit, which caused me no end of embarrassment since I was, you know, an adult at the time.

Rainbowarriors, CocoRosie

CocoRosie's psychadelic imagery and goofy-girly nostalgic sound is charming and everything when you're an American adult woman, but kind of profound when you're, like, a Cambodian teenager really thinking about what the future could be like. The girls I was living with believed in true love, believed that honesty could trump all evil, believed that tigers came out of the forest sometimes to snack on cruel elderly women. OK, that last thing? They believed that because it happened a few months before I arrived in town, and I found out because I make a lot of jokes about women needing sensible shoes in case of tiger attacks, and they didn't go over very well because, as the Cambodian young women explained to me, "if a tiger want to eat you, it will eat you." So in a world where you are approximately as apt to get eaten by a tiger as you are to find a job after college, CocoRosie offers a fairly logical worldview: "If you look hard you can find a / Rainbow trail that's deep inside ya / Fear not you're a rainbowarrior / Goldenlight on everything gleaming." It's a pretty delightful way to think about the world.

We Are Family, Babes in Toyland

God, I was lucky to grow up in the Twin Cities when Babes in Toyland was still around. This punk cover version of the R&B classic is my favorite, ever. I put it on the CD for the Cambodians because they thought Americans were cold since we didn't hold hands everywhere we went together, didn't refer to all our close women friends as sisters, and didn't live with our parents after high school. That all may be true, but I rocked out to this song with a bunch of other losers at a club instead of studying for a math test one night in junior year, and I got the same sense of belonging then as I would, later, walking around Phnom Penh holding hands with my Cambodian sisters.

Monument, Mirah

One of the first rules of the *New Girl Law* was echoed in Mira's amazing, sweet-voiced protest against oppression, which they had been listening to by then for a few weeks: "We have a right to exist, to be free and brave." When we completed the book, it was a simple, hand-bound, letter-pressed, gold silk-covered demand for women's human rights. It didn't go over very well among the older generation of Cambodians, and I had "Monument" on repeat for months to remind me of what mattered when you work with other people.

Hidden Bonus Tracks:
REBEL GIRL, BIKINI KILL
ROCK 'N' ROLL NIGGER, PATTI SMITH
SADNESS OF A KARAOKE GIRL, THE MESSENGER BAND

I tried to play Bikini Kill and Patti Smith for the girls in the dorm once—Heavens to Betsy, L7, and Bratmobile were on that playlist too, natch—but they, well, didn't connect to the rage, righteousness, guitar, growling, or drums. The Cambodian style of promoting women's issues is much more akin to the Messenger Band's "Sadness of a Karaoke Girl," which, in musical style and lyrics, tends toward the pity-laden lachrymose, and is most definitely not how I learned to approach being a girl in a hostile world. Still, I was able to go on tour with the Messenger Band over the winter, and saw that their style of demanding change had an incredible effect. Even if, musically, it was as foreign to me as "Rebel Girl" was to a teenaged Cambodian.

Appendix B
New Girl Laws *(Chbap Srei Tmein)*

---

1) Be patient.

2) Girls should be allowed to choose their marriage partner by themselves, in consultation with their parents.

3) Girls should be educated in schools, alongside boys.

4) Women should have the right to leave the home and join in social activities as men do, or be involved in politics.

5) Girls should be brave enough to make eye contact with and speak to boys.

6) Women should hold positions of power in high society and in politics.

7) Women should be brave, smart, and confident, and should build and strengthen their abilities.

8) Women should learn to protect themselves.

9) Women and men should have access to free high quality education and housing in their home provinces.

10) Women and men should have access to a true democracy and human rights.

11) Women and men should be granted free visas and open borders.

12) Women should have access to free high quality feminine protection.

13) Women and men should be given free health care and preventative health education.

14) In exchange for health care and education, all residents must provide a period of free labor for Cambodia.

15) Domestic violence should be prosecuted and reported by authorities and neighbors, and perpetrators should be punished.

16) Corruption laws should be established, enforced, and respected.

17) A minimum wage should be established for work done in public service.

18) Funding should be established for cultural production.

19) Local production should be supported by reducing taxes and decreasing imports.

20) Laws as written should be enforced by everyone, including lawmakers.

ABOUT THE AUTHOR

Anne Elizabeth Moore is a Fulbright scholar, the *Truthout* columnist behind *Ladydrawers: Gender and Media in the U.S.*, and the author of *Unmarketable* (The New Press, 2007), *Hey Kidz, Buy This Book* (Soft Skull, 2004), and *Cambodian Grrrl* (Cantankerous Titles, 2011), which received a Lowell Thomas Travel Journalism Award. *Hip Hop Apsara* (Green Lantern Press, 2012) is a lyrical collection of photographs and essays from Cambodia.

Co-editor and publisher of now-defunct *Punk Planet* and founding editor of the Best American Comics series from Houghton Mifflin, Moore teaches at the School of the Art Institute of Chicago and works with young women in Cambodia on independent media projects, and people of all ages and genders on media justice work in the U.S. She exhibits her work frequently as conceptual art, has been the subject of two documentary films, and has lectured around the world on independent media, globalization, and women's labor issues. She has written for *The Onion*, *The Baffler*, *The New Inquiry*, *N+1*, *Bitch*, *Tin House*, and *Snap Judgment*. She has twice been noted in the Best American Non-Required Reading series. She is a Fulbright scholar and was a 2012 UN Press Fellow.

Her work with young women in Southeast Asia has been featured in *Time Out Chicago*, *Make/Shift*, *Today's Chicago Woman*, *Windy City Times*, and *Print* magazines, and on *GritTV*, Radio Australia, *Radio K*, and NPR's *Worldview*. She has appeared as a guest on CNN, WBEZ, WNUR, WFMU, and Georgian National television. Her friend the fiction writer Elizabeth Crane wrote a widely reviewed short story about her, thus without knowing it the *Village Voice* called her a "Possibly perfect protagonist"; *Washington City Paper* said she was "A woman who has always been comfortable in her own skin"; and *Hipster Book Club* said she was "A perfect altruistic punk-rock super-heroine." Moore is currently based in Chicago and likes cats and pie.

SUBSCRIBE TO EVERYTHING WE PUBLISH!

Do you love what Microcosm publishes?

Do you want us to publish more great stuff?

Would you like to receive each new title as it's published?

Subscribe as a BFF to our new titles and we'll mail them all to you as they are released!

$10-30/mo, pay what you can afford. Include your t-shirt size and month/date of birthday for a possible surprise! Subscription begins the month after it is purchased.

microcosmpublishing.com/bff